AUTHENTIC

Kat John is a catalyst for transformation, encouraging people to grow beyond external limits and reclaim their authentic selves. Having ignited a ripple effect of empowerment with her signature ZEROFKS movement followed by over half-a-million global fans, Kat inspires others to live boldly, authentically and unapologetically. As an authenticity coach and host of the *Real Raw Relatable* podcast she invites self-discovery, asking people to challenge their limiting beliefs and embrace radical self-acceptance. Leading by example, Kat emboldens her audience to break free from conformity and embrace their true essence with unwavering courage. Guiding souls back to their innate power, she inspires us to lead lives of profound purpose and fulfillment.

katjohn.com.au

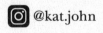 @kat.john

AUTHENTIC

COMING HOME
TO YOUR
TRUE SELF

KAT JOHN

PENGUIN LIFE

UK | USA | Canada | Ireland | Australia
India | New Zealand | South Africa | China

Penguin Life is part of the Penguin Random House group of companies
whose addresses can be found at global.penguinrandomhouse.com

Penguin
Random House
Australia

First published by Penguin Life in 2024

Author photograph © Alexandra Drewniak
Cover design by Alissa Dinallo © Penguin Random House Australia Pty Ltd
Typeset in 11/17 pt ITC New Baskerville by Midland Typesetters, Australia

Printed and bound in Australia by Griffin Press, an accredited
ISO AS/NZS 14001 Environmental Management Systems printer

A catalogue record for this
book is available from the
National Library of Australia

ISBN 978 1 76134 446 6

penguin.com.au

MIX
Paper | Supporting
responsible forestry
FSC® C018684

We at Penguin Random House Australia acknowledge that Aboriginal and
Torres Strait Islander peoples are the Traditional Custodians and the first storytellers of
the lands on which we live and work. We honour Aboriginal and Torres Strait Islander
peoples' continuous connection to Country, waters, skies and communities.
We celebrate Aboriginal and Torres Strait Islander stories, traditions and
living cultures; and we pay our respects to Elders past and present.

Dear Little Kat, we made it, my love, we are home. I know it's been a long journey, and now we get to share it with all the souls seeking to find their way home too. What an honour and privilege!

To those of you seeking to reclaim your authentic self – at times this journey may shake you to the depths of your soul. Stay with it. Hold fast to your inner light and let it guide you home.

Contents

Preface

We cannot know, understand or appreciate peace until it no longer exists within us, because it is only then that we are willing to do anything to get peace back in our lives: peace in our mind, peace in our relationships, peace in our heart, peace in our body.

These words came to me in my mid-twenties as I was sitting in Melbourne's Fitzroy Gardens on a sunny spring day. I'd been struggling to write an essay on 'What peace means to me' and had asked my older brother, Matt, for advice.

'Write from your heart, Neng,' he said, 'from what you've lived.'

So I took myself off to the gardens, took out my pen and started writing from my heart, not my head. I lost myself, in a good way, allowing my words to fill the page without letting my head get too involved. I reflected on the past and the times in my life when it had seemed that peace was nowhere to be found.

If I'd thought it once, then I'd thought it a thousand times – over the first twenty-odd years of my life, I truly believed I had done something majorly bad in a past life or pissed off the karma gods, because my reality up until that point had sucked some serious, major balls. On the surface, everything looked peachy: I grew up with a great family, loving parents, went to good schools, and had a mum who made epic Filipino food. But I was lost.

Maybe you know all too well what I'm talking about here, where you have lost yourself so hard, and been so far away from who you are, that all you can do is be something and someone you know you are not. Grade-A head fuckery. Have you ever felt like being 'you' is simply not enough, or too much, so you don any other kind of persona to be liked and fit in, or find yourself retreating from human connection altogether?

If the answer is yes, then you'll know that no matter how loved-up your family is, or how good a school you go to, or how yum your mum's cooking is, nothing can erase the giant void you feel inside. This, my friends, was my life for the first twenty-four years on this planet. Lost. Inauthentic. Out of touch with my own sense of self, values and truth.

If someone had needed to teach the future generations how to be inauthentic, I'd have been awarded teacher of the century. If there'd been a scholarship for Inauthenticity University, they'd have read my submission and sent me to the front of the line. If there'd been an Olympic medal for inauthenticity, I would have won it! If being inauthentic means being fake, false, dishonest, disingenuous or, more accurately, completely out of touch with who you are, to the point where you act and behave in ways that have zero to do with your true and honest self, then at that time you could have stuck a badge of honour on me declaring I-N-A-U-T-H-E-N-T-I-C in bold letters.

And yet, today, I'm an authenticity coach. I get paid (huh!) to teach people how to come back home to their true selves – a gig I've been doing since 2015 and grow more in love with doing, each and every day. From humble beginnings (like having zero followers and no-idea-how-this-was-ever-gonna-happen kind of humble), my community has grown into the tens of thousands, with hundreds each time participating in my ZEROFKS dance parties and my online and in-person talks and programs. If you'd have told Little Kat that she'd be teaching people around the world how to reclaim their authentic selves, to love themselves and others wholly, and to start living a life filled with deeper meaning and purpose, she would not have known what the hell you were talking about! So how on *earth* did I end up here?

Back then, I didn't know I was acting inauthentic, I thought that's just 'how I was', 'who I was'. As a result, I was a gigantic people pleaser, a burn-the-candle-at-both-ends, don't-need-nobody, I-can-go-it-alone kinda gal. A chameleon. An anxious attacher. A can't-think-or-decide-for-myself, go-with-the-flow person who flowed into places and spaces that were not so great for me. And yet, despite doing all this hard work of trying to be all the things I thought would make people like me more, which should have in turn helped *me* like me more, I hated myself. My self-esteem and self-worth were well below zero, ten feet underground. I was seeking to feel 'good' through being someone I thought the world would like better.

As you'll read in these pages, from the age of six, I lived through some seriously gnarly moments, each one shoving me to a worse place than the last, until one day I was finally shaken *awake*! From then on, I began some intensive inner work, absorbing the teachings of scientific and spiritual gurus and applying them to my own experience. Over a decade, bit by bit, I finally unearthed, released and embraced the real Kat who'd been hiding away all that time. And now, I help others do that too.

I think we all reach this point at some stage – some more intensely than others. In a vulnerable moment we see ourselves . . . catch ourselves in the mirror and momentarily see through who we're pretending to be; not understanding why we're behaving this way and wishing it were different, but with no clue how to change things. In that brief glimpse, you understand that change is coming, destined to make its way through you and your life like a mini – or major – tornado. But nothing quite prepares you for the journey ahead. A journey that will push you to the edge and force you to become *only* who you truly are. It's an almighty journey and a tough one at that, but one that will ultimately bring you home to your authentic self.

If this is a journey you are willing to take, then you've come to the right place. For some reason, you have picked up this book. Something, somewhere deep inside of you, has nudged or even shoved you to take this step. Maybe it's your first step. Maybe you're taking the step again. Either way, deep within is the real you, the one waiting to get out and be seen in daylight – not as someone who exists for others, but as someone who lives for themselves; on their terms, in their way, living their truth. Not the, 'I'm gonna live however I want with zero regard for others, or the planet, or animals, or other people's feelings' kind. And not the, 'this is my life, on my terms, with a shit ton of attitude and deep-seated anger' kind either. No – this is the *considered* life, rooted in heart and in what's right, good and true.

I hope you have found this book before entering a deep, dark spiral, but the sad fact is that many of us must take the hardest path before we can return home to the light. If I can help even one of you avoid the loneliness and naked bathtub of my death-to-ego experience, then I will dance to eternity. But I am also here to say, I understand. If you have gone or are going through the dark night of the soul, you are not alone. I give you my shoulder to lean on, the shared wisdom and experiences of my clients and a carefully considered Mary Poppins bag of useful tools, along with many practical exercises, to help you find your way back to living authentically when you've ventured far from home. On the other side is a life filled with love, laughter and the expression of your true essence. Shall we begin?

Introduction

At school, I felt constantly uncomfortable in my skin. It was as if I were itching to get out of myself, to be *anyone* else but me. Which is why, when I turned eighteen, I let loose – drinking, smoking and partying. I was desperate to break free. At the time, I was studying nursing full-time while living with chronic nerve pain in my shoulder (which would eventually spread throughout my whole body). To try and dull the pain, I was prescribed opioids. They didn't quite hit the spot, but the high was kinda cool. Upgrading to party drugs seemed like a natural step, so I took it.

The first time I took ecstasy, I had a cracking time. As a little girl I'd loved to dance and had taken dance lessons from the age of four. Taking my first pill felt like that pure childhood experience of dancing freely, uninhibited and with absolutely no fucks-in-sight to give. I danced the night away in a pure loved-up state, having an amazing time with my friends. Oh, the freedom, the forgetting of all the junk in my head! It was just too easy for me to fall into taking drugs every weekend and it became a sort of ritual. During the week I studied nursing and worked at a nursing home and on the weekends it was full-time partying. But by 'Terrible Tuesday' each week, the comedown was real. This became my rhythm for about a year and a half.

Initially, I was taking one ecstasy pill when I went out. But as with any addictive substance, you build up a resistance and therefore need more to get the same fix. That was my friends and me.

We started to take an extra half, then an extra three-quarters, then two pills a night. A few of my friends would continue to party on once the club had closed at 6 am. From the Prince nightclub in Melbourne's St Kilda, they'd go to OneSixOne, then move on to Revolver at 9 am to continue partying through Sunday. So, a night that started at 11 pm on Saturday was now moving into the next day. Sounds pretty gross, doesn't it?

I thought so too. So I promised myself that I would never go there, that I would draw the line at 6 am and go home. But the side of me that liked to be liked, to be needed, to be included and be loved, aka Little Miss Needy, adored the fact that my friends wanted me to keep partying with them. It meant that I was 'important', 'cool', 'in' and 'wanted'.

One morning, instead of going home at 6 am, I went back to a hotel room with the crew. There were lines of speed on the table. 'For you!' said my friends.

'No, not a chance am I snorting anything!' I said.

I had vowed I was never going to do 'hard drugs'. But my friends were begging and pleading and, I hate to say it, their puppy dog eyes won me over. I snorted my first line of speed. It gave me the extra pep and energy to keep going and so, of course, I found myself at OneSixOne, and soon after, Revolver. This led to taking even more drugs to 'keep going'. To where, I have no idea. For what legitimate reason, I have not a clue. This turned into coming home Sunday night after a whole twenty-four hours of taking drugs, not sleeping and not eating.

On those Sunday mornings, oblivious to where I was and what I was doing, my beautiful mum would text message me: *I love you, Neng* (my Filipino nickname). Back then, there was no phone tracking and no way for her to know where I was. She had no idea

I was at Revolver, high as a kite, reading her message: I'd feel a pang in my heart, a pain that touched me deep in the well of true knowing. It touched the part of me that wanted to go home, to be wrapped in her safe arms and held. It touched the knowing in me that said I was pushing the envelope too far and knocking on the door of 'shit's gonna get real if you don't stop'. It touched the sense in me that wanted to be honest about the pain and suffering I was living with.

But the outside me, the party-girl me, the I-wanna-be-loved-by-*everyone* me didn't want to hear it, see it, or feel it. Dancing my little drug-addled booty away was all I wanted to care about in that moment. So I would shove my feelings and awareness way, way down. Push them out of mind, out of sight and let the good times roll.

I was becoming too thin, my skin was breaking out, I had constant ulcers in my mouth and the Terrible Tuesday comedowns were getting worse. At university, I wanted to climb out of my skin, desperate to escape my body and how shit I was feeling. But I was in a rhythm, a synced-up routine of going out, partying, recovering, repeat. I was in with the crew, man!

My family were really worried about me, friends who were not in the drug scene were really worried about me, but I didn't give a fuck – and not in the ZEROFKS Tuesday good kind of way. This was the you-don't-get-me-or-my-life kinda fuck, the nor-do-you-get-to-have-a-say-about-how-I-live kind. The not-give-a-fuck with an invisible middle finger shoved right up in their face. The defensive, reckless, chip on the shoulder not-give-a-fuck.

All these people who cared about me would ask after me, a look of desperate concern in their eyes, but I ignored them. I was going to live life *my way*. Forget Little Miss Needy, now Little Miss

Independent wanted to take the stage. And I was lost in the middle. Between these two extremes was the real me – somewhere . . . but I had no idea how to find her, or even if she really existed. These two opposing forces were working double-time against the real me, ensuring she could never see the light of day. I was bouncing back and forth along this scale of people-pleasing to the max on the one hand, and on the other, not caring squat about what anyone else wanted but me. This meant I was constantly making really poor choices and hurting people who loved me and whom I loved too. Most of all, I was hurting myself.

One night I was out partying and this god-awful pain zapped in my shoulder blade. It was killer and I was so uncomfortable. I remember saying to my friend, 'I think I need to go home, this pain is bad!'

She looked at me and said, 'You just need to take another pill.'

Something in me knew that wasn't what I needed. Something in me knew I needed to go home, but the false persona I had built that was so down for pleasing and forgoing my truth took over, so I popped another pill and kept going. Little did I know that the pain in my shoulder would eventually overtake my entire life, my happiness, joy and whole being. Little did I know that chronic nerve pain and opioid dependence would be my next battle – I had another reality check to face first.

Have you had those moments? I bet you have. Those moments when you know in your bones what will serve you, what is best for you, what is right for you, good for you and true for you. But something overrides this, obliterates it as if it never even existed and makes you act, say or do something that temporarily relieves you in the moment, but has you pondering later, *Was that the best choice?*

The peak of my drug taking came one night after a three-day bender. By bender, I mean I hadn't slept, hadn't eaten and had been taking multiple drugs to either stay awake, or get a high, or chill out a little bit, for three days straight. I was staying with a friend, house-sitting her brother's place. Seventy-two hours in, I had no sense of reality. I went into the bathroom, looked at myself in the mirror and did not recognise the person staring back at me. I was looking at my reflection, completely confused, thinking, *Who the fuck are you?* I literally did not recognise my own face. It freaked me out and I started bashing the mirror, yelling, 'Who the fuck are you?' over and over again.

The friends we were hanging out with tried to enter the bathroom, but I'd locked the door. They forced their way in, so I ran out of the bathroom and onto the balcony. I was looking for an escape, any escape, so I thought I should jump. I wasn't thinking clearly – I didn't want to kill myself, I just wanted to get away – the screams in my head and body were deafeningly loud at that point. Nothing made any sense, I didn't know who I was.

My friends grabbed me, put me in a cold bath and sat with me until I came back to reality. Maybe that's why I hate ice baths now. Although my friends were also on drugs, they sobered up pretty quickly. They fed me as I was sitting in the bath, and kept a close eye on me. After a while, one of my friends said, 'Katty, you need help. This is not fun for you anymore, this is a problem. Either we call your brother, or we call your parents to come pick you up.'

It was the last thing I wanted in that moment, but everything I needed. I had stripped myself to raw bone, all my armour gone. I had seen the face of someone I no longer recognised in the mirror. It scared me into stone-cold reality. I had tried to flee, but could not escape. Naked, I had nowhere to hide. Realness and honesty were the only things present – enough to make me want to see, hear and face what was going on underneath. I was being invited by some invisible force to turn within. Every ounce of me wanted to resist its call, but I had no strength left to fight.

PART ONE

HOW WE LOSE OURSELVES

Chapter 1

The ego

Hello me, nice to meet you

It's a precious thing, to know yourself. To have a deep, trusting relationship with our authentic nature and honour its way of wanting to be in the world. Any investment of energy, time and life force into anything other than what is right, good and true for us diminishes our essence. Inauthenticity is a way for our ego to protect itself and try to ensure safety. But there is a price to be paid for that sense of safety, a price that is higher and more harmful than many of us may realise – even as we pay it, year after year.

We come into the world, experience the world, take in the world, create meaning about our experiences, ourselves, others and life, and form an external personality around who we *think* we ought to be. Naturally, through this process, we take the inevitable journey away from our true, real and authentic self. That means bye-bye authentic nature (but hopefully, only for a little while). From the day we're born, we're destined to take this path. But in order to live well, we're also destined to return. Some of us come back sooner. Some of us take the longer route. Some of us don't make it back at all. But the invitation is always there, waiting for your RSVP.

Little Miss People Pleaser

By age twenty-four, I had people-pleased myself so far into oblivion that I didn't recognise myself in a mirror. Shivering near-naked in a bathtub, I had to lose myself in order to find myself. As a kid, before Little Miss People Pleaser took over, I was fancy-free, laughed loudly, was sensitive and intuitive, an extroverted-introvert who had a strong sense of what was going on around me. I was spritely in spirit and filled the room with my energy. I loved to dance, sing and express my emotions with passion. My dad says, 'You were never great at hiding what you were feeling, Neng.' All my emotions were out in the open. I was cute, spunky and, at times, rambunctious.

Then, one traumatic incident changed everything and the confident spark in me started to dwindle. The ease of being me started to fade as the trust I had in the world began to disappear. Rather than acknowledge what had happened (and truthfully, I didn't fully understand it at the time), I began developing armour against the world and walls around my heart – what I now know as 'coping strategies' or, in other words, behavioural tactics to help manage my rising inner angst. At age six, I didn't consciously tell myself to bottle up the experience and keep it hidden away, but subconsciously did so as a means of self-protection. Cue self-destruction, self-hatred and self-abuse. Cue no self-love, no self-respect and no self-belief. Cue people-pleasing on steroids, anxious attachment, misguided anger, disordered eating and drug abuse. Cue the loss of that innocent little girl, the bright spark, the open-hearted spirit. Cue wanting the world to go fuck itself.

This was the beginning of losing myself, hard, for a good decade.

By age fourteen, I had developed obsessive-compulsive tendencies. I was desperately trying to control what I could on the outside because everything on the inside was a big old mess. When your emotions are chaotic, gaining control over something – anything – can bring some peace. Restoring order narrows your focus and lets you feel like the world is okay, at least for that moment. You'll give anything to gain what you think is 100 per cent control over one small thing and do it over and over and over.

For me, that meant rearranging the books on my bookshelf. I'd arrange them in height order, then colour order, then authors' first names in alphabetical order, and then authors' surnames in alphabetical order. Whenever I felt unrest – the uncomfortable tidal wave inside of me – I'd rearrange them again.

After my bookshelf, I'd turn to my wardrobe. 'Okay, cool, let's rearrange my clothes into summer, autumn, winter, spring!' For a moment there they'd be, all ordered, and I'd look at the neat rows and feel like all was well. I'd sigh a sigh of relief, *Ahh, all is a-okay!* A few days would go by and the tidal wave would come back, so I would rearrange my wardrobe from darkest to lightest. Again the tidal wave would return, so I would arrange my clothes from tallest to shortest. But then that would bother me because they were out of colour coordination or out of season coordination. No matter what I did, I couldn't maintain a sense of peace, and so this obsessive-compulsive tendency began to take over my world. I *needed* control. But why?

I remember one night in my bedroom, noticing a folder with a piece of paper hanging out of my school bag. I said to myself, 'Okay, I'm going to test myself and see if I can just let it stay like that.' I went to bed and tried to sleep, but the tidal wave feeling went through my body. It was overwhelming and I felt boiling hot and irritable. As it often did, it jammed up my throat. Because at the time, I didn't know how to deal with these feelings and emotions, the only thing I could do was control my environment. So I got up and fixed the piece of paper in the folder and put it back 'right', thus making the world 'right, in order', a safe place to be again. You can see that I was developing a control dynamic – a practice based on the belief that if I could control my world and environment, nothing bad would ever happen again. This is how coping mechanisms and strategies are born, often from the shit that goes down in early childhood.

The development of the ego

I wasn't born this way. I wasn't born a people pleaser, or a chameleon, or someone who needed to prove I could go it alone, or even a high-flying achiever who didn't know how to rest and actually take a damn chill pill. Neither were you.

These behaviours and personas are birthed, donned and developed unknowingly, and sometimes knowingly, from childhood experiences. We are all born innocent, open-hearted and willing to take in, and take on, the world. Fearless, free, uninhibited. Then life, experiences, trials and tribulations sprinkle, rain or hurricane upon us, moulding and shaping us into an adult who is often far removed from that original sacred space.

We develop an ego as a means of protection. Built from the reactions we have to external experiences, it remembers what happened when it felt embarrassed, shamed, ignored, not enough, or unloved, and it protects us by saying: don't do that again, do this instead, it's safer! We practise responses that help us feel 'safe and secure' and when those responses work, we do them again. For example, if your parent or caregiver was volatile in their moods and this made you feel uneasy and unsafe, maybe the way you

6

helped protect yourself was to keep quiet, to keep the peace and do as they said. And if that response led to you not getting yelled at and kept you out of the firing line, then you can bet your bottom dollar you did it again, and again, and again.

Over time, these behaviours become habits, and when we do them often enough we start to lock them in as part of our 'behavioural identity'. For some people, this looks like always being agreeable, a behaviour initially formed as a way to keep an angry parent happy. For others it could present as the need to take charge of a situation before it takes charge of them. Equally, it could be 'learned helplessness' to encourage others to come to their aid. Or it could be using comedic banter to keep real feelings at bay. These are just some examples of behaviours that become habits, that become personas, that become who we *think* we are, that become who *others* think we are – a tactic your ego uses to keep you feeling safe. And, while the ego is doing all this in an attempt to take care of you, sometimes it can go too far. Initially, the habits it prefers offer a relieving effect, which is why it locks them in. But later, once your life has progressed, if you remain stuck in these behaviours, they can become detrimental.

These personas can help us out, but often they have hidden agendas, seeking their own secret outcomes that have little to do with what your real and genuine self wants. For example, the high-flying achiever can use their drive and ambition to get ahead in their career, do projects around the home or lead a team to great success. But where the hidden agendas come in is when the high-flying achiever seeks to *do* these things to feel enough, to prove they're not a failure, to show others 'look what I've done!'

At this point they become dysfunctional, wearing their burnout as a badge of honour while desperately aching for rest, to be still, to be quiet, to be okay, to just be 'enough'. All too often we become locked into behaviours that are so deeply ingrained, we may not even realise we are stuck in a self that is false. The ego loves certainty and predictability, even if it's costing us our true way.

Your behaviours are the key

I cannot stress enough how vitally important it is to know your ego, your looping stories, wounds, locked-in limited views of yourself, others and life, and the persona you *think* is you, but isn't. Why? Because you are literally making choices every single day from this false self, which has little-to-nothing to do with who you *really* are. I mean, that's gotta scare the shit out of you, right?

My egoic orientation is individualism, with a decent pinch of overpleasing, a sprinkle of overachieving and a dash of needing control. Oh, the joys of managing this! I love to prove to some invisible entity that I can survive and thrive without your help, thank you very much. That I can go it alone and show you (whoever *you* is) that I don't need you.

I also have another persona who attempts to morph into behaving like those around me, to fit in and be liked. This persona likes to scour the room and suss out the 'smart ones', the 'cool ones', the 'in-the-know' ones. It picks up my authentic nature, throws it out of my own body and takes me hostage (at least, it tries to). It'll then decide how to 'best act' in front of these people to 'get in' with them. I mean, fuck, it's exhausting and gross too! The cries of inauthenticity are real! And what a shit way to spend my energy. Deep in my people-pleasing era, I'd start each new day with my energy topped up, only to go off and waste it on either trying to get 'in with the cool kids', or shutting people out. What a ning-nong . . . and yet, this is how I spent the best part of a quarter of a century on planet Earth. 'Like me', 'gotta protect me', 'like me', 'gotta protect me'. That is no way to live and it sure as hell ain't the real Kat.

The work required to get to know both the real *and* the false yous takes some major self-awareness, curiosity and self-responsibility. Among certain people, you want to be aware of your body in space and time. You want to understand what's going on in your head and how that contributes to the way your body behaves in space and time. You want to be curious enough to be like, *Hmm, I wonder why I just said that, why I shut down, why I felt the need to alter myself.* And you want to be self-responsible and enquire deeper; journal, map out your behaviour, note where it links back to and how it's affecting your self-worth, belief, love and respect. It's self-responsible to say, 'I'm gonna do something about this' and take the next best step towards doing something about it.

Get this tool into your life: Enneagram

There are several useful tools to help you understand your personality and take command of your subconscious behaviour patterns. Throughout this book, I'll suggest a variety of tools – ones I use to this day – all tried, tested and loved. One I've found majorly helpful is the Enneagram – a model of the human psyche based upon nine interconnected personality types. Like many such evaluative tools, it can assist in deepening self-awareness, self-understanding and self-development.

Whether using the Enneagram or other tools, spending time reflecting on who you are – both internally and how you show up in the world – is the key to escaping the grip of the ego and embracing your authenticity. A good first step is identifying your fundamental characteristics and default behaviours. If you're keen to get to know yourself better, and I assume you are since you're reading this book, the Enneagram website (enneagraminstitute.com) is a great place to start. It outlines the nine personality types, describing them in detail, how they act out under stress or in growth and how they work with the other personality types. Here's a quick rundown:

#1 The Reformer: rational, idealistic type – principled, purposeful, self-controlled and perfectionistic.

#2 The Helper: caring, interpersonal type – demonstrative, generous, people-pleasing and possessive.

#3 The Achiever: success-oriented, pragmatic type – adaptive, excelling, driven and image-conscious.

#4 The Individualist: sensitive, withdrawn type – expressive, dramatic, self-absorbed and temperamental.

#5 The Investigator: intense, cerebral type – perceptive, innovative, secretive and isolated.

#6 The Loyalist: committed, security-oriented type – engaging, responsible, anxious and suspicious.

#7 The Enthusiast: busy, fun-loving type – spontaneous, versatile, distractible and scattered.

#8 The Challenger: powerful, dominating type – self-confident, decisive, wilful and confrontational.

#9 The Peacemaker: easy-going, self-effacing type – receptive, reassuring, agreeable and complacent.

Now, I'm no Enneagram expert, but having spent some time studying the founders' book, *The Wisdom of the Enneagram*, the Enneagram Institute website and several online programs, I'm now undertaking a formal certification as I truly believe in its value. I regularly apply it to my own and my clients' situations, which is the real test. That's how I love to do the work: I seek to expand myself, am open to learning, find the coach, guide, mentor, book or course, then take it in, let it land and apply it to my life. Once it's grounded in me, I share it with my community as a lived experience rather than a theoretical instruction.

One of the beautiful aspects of the Enneagram is its focus on the *development* of one's persona: understanding that it's not all 'bad', but rather, that the persona operates across levels, expressing itself differently according to how stressed (low levels) or healthy (high levels) a person feels. When we're under duress, we operate from the lowest levels. In this state, working overtime to defend its ego identity, our persona's character can express itself in harmful, destructive and dangerous ways. For example, when operating at the lower levels, #1 The Reformer (aka the rational idealist) can become obsessive about imperfection and others' wrongdoing, while they themselves hypocritically do the opposite of what they preach. At their highest level, the Reformer becomes extraordinarily wise and discerning, accepting what is, instinctively knowing the best action to take in any given moment.

Enneagram work helps us become more self-aware. We can use this knowledge to move our persona into a higher functioning state. In other words, while these behaviours may remain less than ideal and, yes, still driven by ego, we can move the behaviour from total fuckery to less fuckery. Or, as the Enneagram Institute's website explains far more eloquently:

The Levels become a continuous guide to self-observation, a map that we can use to chart where we are in our psycho-spiritual development at any given time. As we move 'up' the Levels, we discover that we are freer and less driven by compulsive, unconscious drives and therefore able to act more effectively in all areas of our lives, including in our relationships.

My predominant persona is Enneagram #4 The Individualist. When I am deep in my shit, aka identified in ego, I will think that there is something very wrong with me, that I am different from everyone else, that my problems and deficiencies are worse than others'. The self-hatred, shame and pity is very real. My feelings are real and become the only thing I rely on, which, especially in that state, is fucking terrible. Steve, my husband, often says, 'My gosh it must be hard to be you when you're in that place!'

Because this Kat ran my life for far longer than I care to admit, I chose relationships that were emotionally unavailable, where I felt I could only share the 'good' aspects of myself and keep the 'bad' ones hidden. When I'd start to let a little more of the 'bad' out, the dudes would magically vanish, time and time again. This persona and pattern ruined my self-esteem and kept me in the same loop for years, reconfirming over and over that there was indeed something very wrong with me. Thus reinforcing the Individualist: the one who thinks they are destined to do life on their own because they're 'so different' from everyone else. That no one gets them or understands them. It's a lonely place.

Meet Katrina

My client Katrina (yes I know it's confusing because our names are similar!) sought her worth in being there for everybody else. Her experience growing up was that men did not show up in a real way for her. Her parents divorced when she was four years old and her mother repartnered soon after. Her father was wounded by this marriage break-up and Katrina clearly remembers the animosity between her parents.

'My sister and I were the collateral damage. Dad was obviously hurt and behaving like a lover scorned and my mum was trying to move on with a new life. I think this is where a lot of my unconscious people-pleasing kicked in . . . to just "be good".'

When Katrina's mother remarried and had another child, all the attention went towards her new half-sister. 'I powered through with being "the good girl" to gain a sense of belonging – or was it simply to just be seen?' Katrina said.

When Katrina was eleven, her mother became unwell. When she was thirteen, her mother sadly died from cancer. Soon after, her step-dad met someone new, remarried and moved overseas. Her real dad also lived overseas. Katrina and her sisters were in the UK and her mother's dying wish was for Katrina and her sisters to stay in the care of her grandparents and aunty in the UK, and so, they did. Neither father figure showed up emotionally, physically or spiritually for her. She was left wondering, *What do I have to do to get the love that I need? Who do I have to be?*

Katrina craved real love. But her younger self had developed a pretty compelling story that she was not worthy and didn't know her place in the world. And so, she met her husband, a man who matched the 'not show up in a real way' story she'd sold herself. More than once, this guy was unfaithful and denied it. He was her perfect 'ego match'. Not chosen by her heart, but by her ego, because it had convinced her that's all she was worth and all she could have.

When she first reached out to me, Katrina wanted to change her work as a high-performing sales manager. She wanted to change the way she lived her life and perhaps look at an alternate career. She was done with working herself to the bone. She wanted more purpose, but she was downright exhausted.

'Of course we can focus on this,' I said, 'but can we go back to the part where you know your husband is cheating on you?'

Katrina didn't want to address that just yet. I said to her, 'There are two giant nut sacks we're looking at here. One is your work, the other is your marriage. And if we're going to work together, *the first thing* we're going to need to look at is your marriage – straight in the eye!'

It didn't take much to recognise that Katrina's Enneagram is #2 The Helper, and that it had overtaken her natural self. Katrina had chosen her husband from her Helper persona, a husband who had cheated on her since day dot, an infidelity she had sensed but could never bring herself to say anything about. They fought. They played tit for tat. They traded needs. They one-upped each other. He cheated on her. She'd bring it up. He'd make her think she was crazy. She'd lose it. He'd say, 'See, you *are* crazy!' She thought she was crazy. She went back into people-pleasing mode. And so it went, on and on . . . until it didn't. Until she couldn't do one more round of it; couldn't pretend anymore, shove it down anymore, lie to herself anymore, stay in that marriage anymore.

So she had *the chat*. The real chat. The, 'You and I both know that this has been over for a long time. I can't go on like this. You can't go on like this. We can't go on like this. Our kids can't keep seeing this,' chat. She was done. She called out the infidelity. She called out their marriage. She called out what she was allowing.

And this was great progress but Katrina still had work to do. As she'd recognised when she first came to see me, Katrina's Helper persona was affecting her career too. She was driving herself well below ground, stretching herself to breaking, just to show others, 'See, I'm worthy; see, I did good, right?' She was tied up in so much good-girling – hoping that it would stop her husband cheating, or prompt her boss to say, 'Wow, you're amazing, you're such a trouper.' But at what cost?

Katrina put her hand up for a voluntary redundancy and took some months off to absorb her brave move in addressing the two giant nut sacks in her life. In time, she created her own consultancy business, backing herself to do what she was good at, at her pace, her rhythm. A company she was contracting for had two head honchos and one of them had been giving her an especially hard time. He was constantly on her case about hours, money and performance and often belittled her work by saying things like, 'Why does this EDM strategy and delivery cost so much? I'm sure anyone could do this for half the price!'

She was in all sorts about it because her ego stories had flared up again. The stories went a lot like this: *I don't know what I'm doing, I need to charge less, my work isn't good enough, why did I leave my corporate job? I need to get a real job and not do this business anymore.*

Her behaviour went into over-giving herself, over-nicing herself, aka overcompensating. Her client's way of operating in the world (no doubt fuelled by his own persona) flicked at her wounds, woke up her limited view of herself, turned on her Helper persona switch and voilà, the cycle began again.

As we'd been working together for two years, Katrina knew she had reverted to Helper mode, knew she was spinning in her old ways, and knew she needed to end this behaviour. The timeframe between being able to recognise her dysfunctional Helper behaviour and being able to shift back into her authentic self had decreased dramatically from when I first met her. She was noticing, observing and watching herself the whole time, aware of what she was doing, and went into her values work to plug back into her authentic ways. By the time she came to her coaching session, she had identified the problem, brought herself back home and only required some additional support and guidance for the next steps in how to approach this idiot, while keeping her authentic self intact.

Katrina asked herself one good question. 'If I stayed *me* in this scenario, what would I do and what wouldn't I do?'

Chapter 2

Threats to living authentically

Why is it so important to know your ego?

Imagine for a moment the real cost that suppressing our true self puts on our spiritual, mental, emotional and physical wellbeing. Imagine what takes place inside of us when we morph, contort, hide or overcompensate due to our ego telling us we can't be ourselves or do life the way we want to.

I don't mean in a selfish, 'I'll do life my way and you can all go fuck yourselves if you don't like it!' way. I'm not talking about that and never will be. I'm talking about the way our hearts are beckoning us to live our lives *our* way. The amount of energy that goes into repressing our authentic nature in order to forget who we truly are is enormous. Imagine what we could bring about in our lives and the wider impact that could have, if we refocused that energy towards something good? What joy, wisdom, light, peace and contentment would await you?

It's beautiful! And I'd love to tell you that once you find yourself the work is done, but it's never done. Having a healthy relationship with your ego is an ongoing dance. But the dance, too, is beautiful!

Glimpses of the past

I was a good kid. I made friends easily. I was likeable, friendly and I existed to please others. Well, that's what I thought anyway. I didn't think about myself or what I wanted. I did everything necessary to fit in, to feel that I was liked, to feel that I was loved. Sure, I was popular, but man, it was stressful. I would turn myself into whoever or whatever others needed me to be. Like a people-pleasing pretzel, I would bend and contort into every manner of shape and form. 'Oh, you need me to be like this, sure, I can be like that!'

I did whatever I was told to do, or what I thought I should do, to make myself popular. I stepped on others to lift myself up. I created cliques and said whatever enabled me to get 'in' with the cool crowd. My behaviour was the epitome of someone who didn't respect herself or others, driven by this invisible but oh-so-real need to fit in. It was a survival mechanism, one I'm not proud of, but *why* was I doing this? What was underneath it all?

My #2 Helper aka Pleaser mode is a behaviour I play out when my #4 Individualist is sitting in the average-to-unhealthy levels (ego town). Meaning, when I'm stressed out or not in control of a situation, I'll shift to the unhealthy behaviours of the Pleaser and push myself up in everyone's grill to be liked. A hidden agenda at play. Yeah, I know, head fuck. Our patterned responses are dynamic, but at the same time, they're also predictable.

One day, at school, I would have been around twelve years old, a flashback of what happened when I was six entered my brain. Her searching hands, her lips and breath. Her nakedness. It was just a series of confusing glimpses which both did and did not stack up, and it shocked me. *What the hell is that?* Up until that point, I hadn't remembered anything so vivid. It didn't seem to make sense, yet, deep down, *I knew*. The part of me that wanted to forget, suddenly remembered. I remembered it all – and I felt sick. It was a moment that reminded me *not* to forget, *not* to let this go, *not* to let this slip by the wayside. I couldn't ignore the truth of what happened, what I saw and how I felt. The memory had surfaced for good, and now it was in my hands. What was I to do with it? I had two choices: deal with it or let it deal with me.

Tentatively, I shared my memory with two trusted people. Sadly, and perhaps it was as much 'the age' as 'our age' – of believing that denial and ignorance was the best way to move forward – they both dismissed it as nothing to worry about and suggested I'd mis-remembered. I *so* wanted to believe them. So I did. Or at least, I tried to. I wasn't quite convinced, but I convinced myself enough. *Yeah, you're right, it wasn't that bad, it probably was my imagination, I probably did make it up.*

Environment, society and culture

From the ages of zero to seven we rapidly absorb the world with our subconscious mind, sponging up incoming information from our environment, both positive and negative. It's widely accepted that the subconscious mind is inaccessible to your conscious mind but that it affects your behaviour and emotional learning. During our early years, our upbringing, home environment, parents, care-givers, siblings, pre-school, TV shows and their messaging play a big role in forming our identity, their effects becoming increasingly visible after seven years of age.

Now, I'm not a biological parent, but I am a step-parent (or 'bonus mum' for a more positive spin on the dreaded step-mother title). I've been in my bonus daughters' lives since they were seven and nine years old, and I can tell you from first-hand observation that what they absorbed in their first seven years watching, noticing, observing and mimicking, has only intensified with each birthday thereafter.

Personality traits, outlooks and behaviours that were there when they were younger – power plays, responses, reactions, ways to get their needs met, et cetera – continued to develop and, by the time they were teenagers, became fully formed, locked-in views of themselves, others and the world. Little things that had shown up when they were younger became clearly obvious around the dinner table when they reached their teens – from the way they viewed love, went about getting love and pushing away love, to the way they viewed friendships, intimate relationships, marriage, money, health, their appearance, the lot.

It's clear to me the difference between what's been imprinted on them and how it's shaped their outlook versus their real truth. The same goes for your parents, their parents, you, your children, your nieces and nephews, and your friends. And for me too. No one gets out of the first seven years of life without being affected by their surroundings – the people in their lives and the (not so) subtle messaging around them, coming from marketers, commercials, magazines and now, social media.

When I was growing up, my mum wasn't keen on me buying or reading *Dolly* magazine, due to her concerns about the images I'd see of the models and how sharply I'd compare myself to them. 'How come they don't have pimples? How come they don't have fat knees? How come they have blonde hair and I have poo-brown auburn hair? How come they are really tall? What do they eat to be that skinny? What *don't* they eat to be that skinny?'

Mum had a great point when it came to not wanting me to see those magazines. But I'd see them at the checkout counter or at a friend's place and the comparisons would begin. *That's how I should look, so why don't I? How can I? How will I?*

Bye-bye, authentic Kat. Hello, stronger development of ego.

'Authentic self' versus 'ego self'

We move away from our authentic nature because the personas we develop (unknowingly at the time) help us 'make it through' life. Particularly during our first seven years on the planet, we create various personas to cope, manage and compensate for reality and our experience of reality. We edit ourselves because 'that' aspect of us is too weak, or we didn't get the response we thought we'd get, or we copped shit for being a 'know-it-all'.

With each new persona, we cover up our authentic nature and anaesthetise it for as long as we can. We wear these masks to work, on dates, to interviews, and when we meet people for the first time, ready and armed to present 'me'. The ego uses your persona as a shield, to protect you from the 'big bad world' and all the potential dangers it presents. Its motivation is sound, but its execution can leave a lot to be desired.

Persona, by definition, is the *aspect of someone's character that is presented to or perceived by others*. It's an act or behaviour we don, use to describe ourselves, behave in accordance with, and present as our way of being in the world. As such, the world knows you as *this*, reinforces that you are *this* and so, you stay true to *this* persona, thinking it's actually 'you'. Part and parcel of being human is to have an ego and a persona (jackpot! Not). No one can escape it and it's no use pretending otherwise. As you form your identity over the first seven years of your life, the ego's role is to keep you within that identity and discern what is safe or not safe to go for, let in or experience for that identity to not be disrupted.

This is why we end up in relationships that don't serve the real us. We get together with someone based on who we *think* we are, not who we *actually* are. If your persona, like my client Katrina's, is a Helper, you will choose someone who responds to this need in you. But as an aware adult, you have the right (and responsibility) to ask yourself if that's the dynamic you truly want in your lifelong partnership. Being aware of your dominant operating persona will invite you into the world of healing – to look at the wounded younger self who is playing the lead role in your adult life, acknowledge their pain, their reasoning for thinking, *This is how we have to be*, and have a chat with that younger self. When you do this you will release the ego's hold on you and operate with greater choice to support your authentic self.

There's a person in my life who, before I see them, makes me quite literally want to crawl into myself, fold myself up and over a gazillion times and disappear. That's my automatic response. My head tells me they're much more powerful than me, that it's better to keep them happy and have them like me. Now, this person is closely identified with their ego and is quite difficult to be around, so I'm sure I'm not the only one who reacts to them in this way. When I was stuck in my people-pleasing state, whenever I would see them, I'd find myself morphing into their temperament, their conversations, their Debbie Downer vibe to simply 'make it easier'. Only when they left could I breathe and finally unfold myself and crawl back out into the light.

Once I realised this was happening, it made me hella curious about why I felt the need to do that and which part of me that feeling was coming from. I soon recognised the old, wounded Kat inside who needed to behave that way. Giving into her would have meant overriding the good work I'd done to unearth the real me and I was no longer prepared to give old Kat the reins.

Get this tool into your life: Check Your Reponse

Where do you notice yourself acting in a way that diminishes your true nature? What people or places make you want to crawl inside yourself, or jump outside yourself, aka abandon ship and be overtaken by a false you?

Maybe you're downright exhausted, you've worked long days all week, you're looking forward to a Friday night in – introverted time, face mask, delicious dinner, candles lit and your favourite movie. As you're leaving the office, a friend says she needs you and invites you over for pizza and wine. In other words, wants your ear and energy until midnight. Do you:

1. Without hesitation write back, 'Sure, what can I bring?'
2. Tell her some elaborate lie about needing to work all weekend because it's easier to blame it on work than claim self-care.
3. Pretend you never saw the message so you don't have to come up with a reply in the moment, then deal with it tomorrow.
4. Text a sad-faced emoji along with, 'Hope you're okay, my love. I'd love to be there for you tonight but I'm heading home for some self-care, it's been a big week. How about Monday after work?'

If this were a *Cleo* magazine article, I would provide you with a scoresheet indicating your personality based on your answers. But the truth is a little more complex than that. I'm far more interested in the truth *behind* your decision. Did you say 'yes' because you were genuinely in the mood to be there for your mate, or because you felt obliged? Did you overdo the enthusiasm because that's your nature or because you believe you have a deficiency to make up for? When being curious about getting to the source of whether your behaviours are ego-driven or birthed from your authentic self, it's important to be aware of your underlying motivations and how these decisions make you feel – both in the moment and in the longer term.

Meet Libby

I coach many women who got married when they were young because it was the 'thing to do'. Whose thing? Who made the timeline to get married at an age where you're very much still finding out who the fuck you are, who you're not, what you want and what you don't want? I don't know the answer. I even googled 'why did people back in the day get married young?' What I read didn't make it any clearer to me why the societal pressure was there in the first place.

When we met, my client Libby said that she'd never stopped to ask herself if she ever wanted the whole happily-ever-after marriage story. She'd been twenty-three when she got engaged, twenty-five when she had their first child, thirty when she had their second and thirty-nine when she walked into my world begging for me to help her find herself. Her marriage had no pulse. The silence between Libby and her husband was deafening. Their unspoken words weighed down their home and there was barely any space to breathe. Their sex life, gone. Their eye contact, minimal. Their desperation for the other to speak and say, 'This isn't working, is it?' was palpable. But no one would utter a damn word. It was off to weekend sports like everything was fine and dandy. Off to birthdays, weddings, funerals (or whatever gathering) side by side, but not hand in hand. Libby ached for an alternate life. She ached for another man's touch. She ached for something or someone to swoop in, take away the pain and suffering and enable her to live for herself.

Libby grew up under her mother's thumb, a woman who lived by doing things *the right way*. The conventional way. The don't-do-anything-that-will-spark-questions-or-draw-attention way. The make sure you get married, have children, have more children, be there for your children, always, and don't-make-so-much-as-a-squeak-about-it way. The *I CAN'T FUCKING BREATHE* way.

'Kat,' Libby said to me, 'if I had my time again, I wouldn't do it. This life that I'm in, I don't believe it was meant to be mine.'

The pain in her words sent a dagger into my heart. It took real courage for Libby to let those words out of her swamp of shame and be heard by someone else.

One of the tools I used with Libby was Future You, a tool that calls in your next layer of self to offer up guidance, a next best step to take towards the truth. Libby's future self silenced the noise with its simplicity. It grounded her and reminded her where her path was. It eased the angst with one simple next best step. It's an integral practice that keeps you plugged into your core self, nurturing your intuition and backing yourself. I asked Libby to close her eyes and open up her imagination as I spoke these words:

Imagine that somewhere in your future there is a you who is grounded in
who they are, knows who they are, is connected to their intuition and true

self, and who is so goddamn real and genuine that they ooze that special something.

Imagine how free and liberated that version of you must be and how ace they are at navigating their own mind, ego trip-wires and patterned responses.

Imagine how cool must it be for them that they get to choose how they want to be rather than be who they think they have to be.

We paused for a moment. Libby could feel the presence of her future self right there with her. But there was more to come. I continued:

Now, imagine never meeting them.

Imagine if you never gave them the chance to go out into the world and play, meet people, call in opportunities and dance with life from that place.

Imagine if they were there, waiting, until you took your very last breath without ever having had the chance to do and create life from that place.

Don't let that be your reality or regret. Go and meet them, now.

When Libby opened her eyes, tears streamed down her cheeks. Tears of grief for the lost Libby she had left unclaimed. Tears of joy for the future Libby she imagined becoming. Tears of peace for the woman she was now choosing to honour.

This could be you, too. Just imagine.

Chapter 3

Losing your way

Ego is the armour

As we move through the world, we are inevitably shaped by our experiences – the challenges we face, the traumas we endure and the societal pressures we navigate. These external forces leave an indelible mark on our psyche, shaping the development of our protective ego as a means of coping and survival.

From a young age, we are bombarded with messages and expectations – from family dynamics and cultural norms to social standards and media influences. Such forces mould our perceptions of ourselves and others, honing the lens through which we view the world and influencing the formation of our ego.

Environmental stresses and traumas, whether they stem from childhood experiences, interpersonal relationships or broader issues, can have a profound impact on the development of our ego. They can trigger a range of emotional responses, from fear and anxiety to anger and despair, leading us to erect barriers and defences as a means of self-preservation.

For many of us, the ego serves as a protective shield against the perceived threats of the world – a means of buffering ourselves from pain, rejection and vulnerability. It operates on autopilot, employing a range of defence mechanisms and coping strategies to navigate the complexities of life and shield us from harm.

While the ego may serve as a vital function in the short term, allowing us to survive and adapt to challenging circumstances, it can also hinder growth and self-actualisation. It can trap us in patterns of thought and behaviour that no longer serve us, perpetuating cycles of fear, limitation and self-sabotage.

By gaining a deeper understanding of the forces that shape our ego, we can begin to unravel its grip on our lives and move towards liberation.

Who put this Kat in charge?

As well as the OCD tendencies I developed as a teenager – obsessively ordering my bookshelves and my wardrobe – I also sought control through binge eating. It's like the tidal wave of emotions 'made me' eat my feelings, and because I would feel not only full, but repulsed with myself, I would then have to throw up. When I tell you I hated myself, I mean it. I hated the way I looked, I hated my body, I hated the shape of my face, I hated my hair.

I actually don't recall how long I binged and purged, but I do remember my Aunty Julie as being my saving grace. She picked up on my behaviour one time when I was staying at her place – I often went there to take a break from my parents – and she helped level me out and bring me back to reality when my thoughts were taking me into the pits of darkness.

Anyone who has experienced any type of trauma that shocks them out of their safe little bubble, their safe and trusting view of the world, will know about these kinds of coping strategies. And you know what? You don't even need to have experienced trauma to develop coping strategies. We *all* do it. Some cope through watching porn or paying for sex, some through spending money and racking up credit card debts, others through mindlessly scrolling social media, through self-harm, alcohol abuse, overworking or any number of ways of numbing yourself.

We come into the world as our natural selves, born into families and societies that have their own view of how life should work and how you should work in it. Our parents' expectations of being excellent will mean you develop coping strategies. Society's expectations about behaving appropriately will mean you develop coping strategies. These strategies lead us to develop coping mechanisms that give us a false sense of security, a false sense of control, a false sense of safety. What we're really dealing with is a lot of anxiety about reality and about what might happen if we aren't excellent or well behaved. Or, what might happen if we speak our truth and disrupt parental expectations and the 'appropriate' norms.

As a result, we start to develop tendencies that, over time, solidify into our perceived personalities – personas that aren't actually us. We develop an outer shell for the world and that's how the world knows us. People start to say things like, 'Oh yeah, they're a high achiever' or, 'Oh yeah, they're always there when you need them' or, 'Oh yeah, they'll stay back if you ask them to' or, 'Oh yeah, they're overbearing' or, 'Oh yeah, they have trust issues, trust me'. This is how people come to know us, but it's not *really* who we are.

Around the time I was binge eating, a good friend said she'd noticed that I was really angry. She asked me, 'What's going on, what's happening for you? You seem angry and agitated and are lashing out all the time.' I felt I could share what had happened when I was a little girl. My friend said that I needed to talk to someone, that I should go and speak to the school counsellor. At our school, the counsellor was also our art teacher and she was a pretty cool chick. So I listened to my friend and I made an appointment.

For the first time since I'd mentioned my flashback to my friends, I found myself telling someone else what I remembered experiencing at age six. This time, my feelings were validated. The counsellor helped me to see that I could trust my own memories and intuition. She confirmed that the girl I recalled had attended the same school. She described her as 'disturbed, a loner, someone who was a bully, but also a girl who was in great pain and internally conflicted'. The counsellor explained that the girl had trouble at home and brought that trouble to school and put it onto other people.

From that moment, I started to feel that I could trust myself and my feelings. I started to learn that, although I was caught up in shame and guilt, these emotions were a normal response and that my best path of action was to acknowledge, address and deal with them. Unfortunately, however, my ways of dealing with them remained self-destructive for some time yet.

Lived and intergenerational trauma

Trauma has become a bit of a buzzword on social media these days, which is both great and gives me the ick. Great, because it's made people more aware of how pervasive and persistent trauma is and given us some vocabulary to talk about it. And ick, because in making trauma seem so common, its real impact may not be taken seriously, and can be misused and weaponised. Gabor Maté and The Holistic Psychologist are absolute guiding lights when it comes to trauma, trauma responses and how to heal. If you're not across their work, get across it. On the other hand social media encourages flippant comments like, 'Oh, don't do that, it's traumatising', when someone is just chewing gum or eating a banana. In these instances, using words like 'trauma' when we're simply annoyed or irritated and want to control a situation is not helpful for anyone. Nevertheless, I think we all understand that catastrophic life events and circumstances, such as being physically, sexually or emotionally violated, losing a loved one, or wide-reaching environmental or social disasters, have traumatic effects on people both in the moment and throughout their lives. Sometimes, the effects carry on down through the generations.

Steve, my beloved, when rooted in his authentic nature, is a giant Care Bear. I actually bought him a Care Bear for his birthday a few years ago as a totem to remind him of who he really is underneath his external armour. His persona is Enneagram #8 The Challenger, the ultimate 'don't you dare even think about fucking with me, because I'll fuck you back with ten times the power'. When he's operating in his higher power, he is generous, loving, caring and genuinely enjoys being there for his people, his family. However, his egoic orientation is *consumed* with power – and not in a good way. When this manifests, he needs to be in control, to have the upper hand and not appear weak. He cannot risk being taken down by others. Why does he have this orientation? What did he take in, absorb, experience and make it all mean which can cause him to venture so far from himself?

Steve has inherited family trauma – also known as intergenerational trauma – best defined as psychological and emotional wounds that have accumulated over time and transferred to future generations. During the Second World War, Steve's grandfather was sent to a labour camp and his grandmother was in the concentration camp in Auschwitz. During this experience, her power, independence and humanness were taken, which made her very hard and controlling. As the matriarch of the family, she strived to maintain order and was conditional with her love. This trauma-induced protection mechanism created many rifts within the family, often causing family members to be ousted for periods of time. She received no consequences for her behaviour – the family never dared to question her authority, and instead sought her acceptance. When Steve was in primary school Steve's grandmother called him 'Mr Average' due to his 'average' school grades, while heaping loving praise on his brother for his good grades, as the family sat around the dinner table. Steve recalls how no one came to his defence during these exchanges and how powerless, weak and vulnerable he felt.

Little Steve experienced these situations, took in the information, absorbed it and gave it meaning. To him, it meant that others have the ability to overpower you and your family, and make you feel like you're nothing but a piece of shit. This created an emotional wound that carried deep pain and fed the ego. In order to 'get rid of' that pain or, at the very least, compensate for it, Little Steve (subconsciously) made a decision to never again let anyone have that kind of power or control over him, his family or how he feels. Now, of course, living in the world that we do, that simply is not possible. But for a very long time, his persona, like his grandmother's, told him to lock his heart, never let his guard down and always, always have the upper hand. But at what cost?

You can't outrun the bear

Trauma is not only inherited. Sadly, everyday life can generate a constantly activated stress response. Many people are living with anxiety and overwhelm on a daily basis. It's important to learn to recognise this and find ways to manage it. Taking care of yourself can help alleviate the pressures of long-term chronic stress but it doesn't mean you can avoid shocks to your system. Being human means we are continually bombarded with things that pressurise our days. The most important thing is how we deal with them.

In 2023, Steve and I went for a walk by the beach. I'd planned to go to the gym that morning, but had slept poorly, so decided to give my body a rest. Steve suggested we walk the canals but it was such a beautiful morning that I said, 'Let's do the beach!'

As we were walking home, we came across a group of people surrounding a man on the ground. My nurse instincts turned on as I realised they were giving him CPR. I gave the dogs to Steve and walked towards the group, calmly assessing the situation as I got closer, mentally running through the first-aid DRSABCD method (Danger, Response, Send for help, Airway, Breathing, Cardiopulmonary resuscitation, Defibrillate) – the recommended initial response to treat someone who's suffering a medical emergency.

A friend of ours was among the group and recognised me. 'Kat was a nurse!' she said. The lady who was doing CPR immediately made way for me to take over. We could hear ambulance sirens in the distance but the man on the ground was non-responsive. His skin was pale, grey and clammy. His eyes were fixed. I thought to myself, *Fuck, we're in some serious trouble here.* I kept up CPR, he took a gigantic breath and everyone gasped. He was responsive.

The ambos soon arrived and told me, 'Keep going!' as they got organised. Finally they took over and took the man to hospital. It was unclear whether he was going to be okay.

For two weeks afterwards, I was out of it. I was exhausted, sleeping non-stop and unable to focus. I felt numb but had deep emotions swirling inside me. Each time I'd leave the house for a walk and see a man running, I'd think, *Get ready in case they need CPR*. I'd look closely at their skin colour as they passed and listen out after them in case they fell. Walking past the spot where the CPR had taken place made my heart race and my breath quicken. It made me super alert. I had to cancel coaching sessions, postpone dinner plans and extend deadlines.

Knowing all that I know, it should have been obvious that I was experiencing a state of post-traumatic stress. But I didn't want to believe it or admit it. I didn't want to make a big deal of it. I wasn't the one who'd had the heart attack and whose life would change from that moment on. But my mind kept buzzing and my body was not working properly. Theoretically I understood the signs, but our minds aren't always rational, and mine had trapped me in a state of hypervigilance.

It took a dear friend of mine who is a psychotherapist to point out what was going on. He told me to, 'Ground the fuck down' and reminded me to focus on processing the experience with as little noise and distraction as possible. He told me to stop finding things to do and instead 'sit in' my feelings and work through whatever came up – sit in the sun, sleep in the sun, feel whatever macro or micro emotion is there, let it be there and give it a moment. When I finally did as he instructed, I cried. I let it out. Only then could I acknowledge the enormity of the moment that all of us on the beach had experienced that morning. Only then could I come out of the stress response and into healing, into reintegration.

The man survived. We connected through our local Facebook group and had breakfast, eight weeks later. Every day I wear the heart necklace around my neck that his family gave me to say thank you. Every now and then I wonder how he's doing.

Get this tool into your life: Pain Kicker

How do you make the pain, the unease, the ick, the fiery anger, the pits of shame go away? What's your strategy? Sometimes we rely on less helpful tactics like shopping, eating, or tidying (guilty!) to subdue the pain. Another common approach is to lash out at or withdraw from those we care about. Ultimately, these tactics can make you feel worse, not better. You end up dealing with how shit you feel about yourself rather than what's actually going on. Becoming more aware of when your emotional pain gets triggered – where it sits in your body and how it makes you feel – and then taking a proactive approach to soothing it in more supportive ways can be a game changer. But how the hell do we do that?

1) **Acknowledge a painful moment.** Think back to a time when you were triggered and experienced charged thoughts. Pull out your journal, name the situation and spend some time writing down what went through your mind in that moment.

2) **Name the pain.** Now, describe the feelings and emotions you experienced so your pain is no longer in the dark. Name where it showed up in your body and how it felt – hot, cold, stuck, swollen? Some people see it in colours, or feel it as sensations, or even hear it as sounds. Try to describe the pain using your senses. This is our

brain's way of trying to physicalise a feeling. Once you've identified it in this way, it can be easier to recognise it again in the future.

3) Notice how you resolved the pain. In other words, how did you make the pain go away? Did you collude with others and try to get them on your side? Disconnect, withdraw and withhold your love, kindness, care and choose to wallow in victimhood? Become overbearing or dominant, a spitfire with your words, to push people away? Turn your attention to physical tasks like eating, shopping or ferociously cleaning the kitchen bench and sink so there are no water beads left? Numb out with substances, addictions or unhelpful behaviours? While these tactics might make you feel better in the short term, they are all ways of numbing out, being avoidant and disengaging from the real issue. Instead of acknowledging and addressing your feelings, you're kicking the can down the road.

4) Find another way. In this fourth and final step, write out a healthier response to your pain. I'm not asking you to avoid it or pretend it doesn't exist, rather embrace it and find a better way to process it. Ten times out of ten, the situation requires presence, which helps create space between you and what set you off, allowing for a better choice, another way. Instead of yelling at your partner, could you acknowledge that you need a moment and step away? Instead of mindlessly eating your feelings, could you take a walk around the block and give your emotions a minute to be felt? Instead of freezing out your friend, could you write them a letter that maybe you don't even send? Moving your body often helps, which is why I dance so much.

I want to make it super clear that I am not talking about situations and scenarios where someone is in danger, at risk of physical or sexual abuse, for example. In those moments I very much appreciate and respect that you do what you gotta do, quite literally, to survive. What I'm talking about here are normal-life situations that see you overreact, so you spiral out of control and into the depths of despair. Like when you've gone on a date and the person doesn't call you back in the time you'd hoped. Or when you've started a new business and prepped as much as you can for the launch, and no one buys your service or product in the time you'd hoped. Or when your partner comes home from work in a filthy mood after you've made the house nice, made dinner and, by your account, set up a night of intimacy and connection. Or when you've delivered a presentation that you worked your arse off for and your manager was on their phone not paying attention. Or when you chose not to drink and rocked up to your friend's birthday and people kept hassling you, saying, 'Just have one drink, loosen up a little, it's for so-and-so's birthday, don't be rude!'

Meet Tina

Externally, Tina's life was perfect. Perfect family, perfect home, perfect children, perfect everything. She had the kind of life you'd write about in your journal in the hope of manifesting it one day. At least, that's how it looked on the outside.

In her heyday, Tina fell head over heels for a man whilst on teaching rounds overseas. Upon her return they stayed in contact and he planned to visit, but her family saw no point in this and wouldn't allow it. She contemplated travelling back to see him but felt guilty for potentially going against her family. She listened to them over her own truth, and 'got on' with life as she knew it. Fast forward a couple of years to where she ended up marrying another man who would repeatedly cheat on her and lie to her face if she approached him about it. She tried seeing therapists, but no one seemed to understand her, nor the complexity of the relationship. When her husband would join in therapy sessions, he would continue to baffle with his bullshit lies.

Tina lived like this for twenty-five years. Twenty-five years in a giant lie that she felt the need to hide. She protected her life and daughters with perfection so no one would question it. But the years took their toll. Between her good-girl coping strategy and perfectionist coping strategy, Tina was crumbling. And we all know that we can only put up a façade for so long before it gets too heavy, too burdensome, too suffocating.

Tina's fear in leaving her husband was linked to the fear of opening up her life for the world to see it all: their mess, their secrets, their imperfections. Tina had protected her husband for so long, she feared looking like a fool who had stayed and stood by him. Or worse, what if no one believed her and called her crazy? She was also afraid that by staying she'd never be able to look at herself in the mirror and love herself, respect herself and recognise herself. That the spark she'd seen diminish over the years – her spirit, her essence – would finally be extinguished and she'd become a shell of a woman who had buried the truth to keep her husband out of the firing line.

Fuck, it's all too common, isn't it? Burying our truth, hiding what feels right for us, good for us, true for us from ourselves and being dishonest and lying to ourselves to keep the order. But whose order are we adhering to? And how is it affecting our lives and who we *really* are?

There was no denying that if Tina were to leave, there was a lot on the line. What if her girls sided with their dad? Where would she live? How would she go about buying or renting a house? What would she do for money? She hadn't worked for almost eighteen years, in order to raise their girls. Would she ever meet someone new? What if she were alone for the rest of her life? All their finances were managed by her husband, plus she had been married since her early twenties, so the thought of being solo in the world and the leader and champion of her own life both excited her and scared the living shit out of her. All the stories running around in her head like wildfire kept her in doubt and, at times, convinced her that 'it's not that bad'.

Haven't we all done that?

But if Tina stayed, *everything* was on the line. Her sense of self, gone. Her intuition, silenced. Her self-worth, sub ground level. Her desires, longings, yearnings from the depths of her heart, buried.

During our six months of working together, Tina came to terms with what was on the line, trying to figure out which option was worse than the other. Deep down, she knew. Underneath 'it's not that bad' was a resounding truth, so real and so honest, that in time, she realised she couldn't fight it anymore. In time, her moment would come to be real and honest with not only herself, but the people in her life. In time, shit was going to get very real and birth authentic Tina. In our sessions, that is the space I held for her. She already knew the truth, what she needed was a safe space to unravel it.

It took Tina twenty-five years for that truth to make its way into her full-blown awareness where no amount of fighting it with per-fection could shove it back inside. Just because we become aware of a hidden truth after years of repression, doesn't mean we're willing and ready to act upon it the next day and reorganise our lives. I mean yes, that can happen, but longstanding hidden truths need time to process. You need to sit with them awhile before making a move. Some may think that sounds like self-sabotage or being indecisive, but I believe it's a necessary step in the process of becoming more real and authentic. It's a step to honour and respect, as it's a big moment of being honest with yourself. It's a step where grief starts to take place because you know, deep down, that the life you've been living, and how you've been showing up in it, is about to change.

Tina left her husband. She weathered people's questions, concerns and surprised reactions. She weathered his family's remarks about the marriage and their lack of support once the truth was out. She weathered his commentary, his disbelief in what she'd 'done to him'. She weathered her daughters' emotions and confusion around the end of the marriage. She weathered real estate agents' appointments, the selling of their family home, legal settlement, becoming financially independent and finding a new place to live. She got rained on, hailed on, snowed on, hurricaned on, windswept on. She weathered a great storm for two years to break free from twenty-five years of holding her truth, her soul, her spark, her spirit and her authentic self, captive.

Of course, she wondered if it was all worth it. She doubted her ability to hold it all and surrender to it all. She questioned if what she was doing was right. Amid the shit storm she weathered not only others' concerns, but her own ego's relentless attempts to have her drop it all and go back to what she knew.

Once the dust had settled and Tina had moved into her beautiful new apartment, she invited me and a few other clients of mine she had made friends with over for dinner. Her daughters were there too. She'd done it! She was living solo, finding her feet in the world as her authentic self with her soul and her spirit intact. It was a beautiful sight. On her balcony, as we watched the sun go down, we raised a toast to her and to all those who had stepped up and been there for her in one way or another during the 'unravelling'. The storm she had weathered was worth it. She was *home*.

Chapter 4

Coping strategies

Content warning: this chapter contains discussion of
self-harm and suicide. Please read with care.

Which master are you serving?

Let's start with a simple truth: we *all* have our coping strategies.
Whether consciously or unconsciously, they're ingrained in the
fabric of our existence. But why do we rely on them so much? The
answer lies in our shared human experience – particularly our
journey from childhood to adulthood.

As children, we are sent into a world brimming with people,
emotions and challenges that often exceed our capacity to take
them all in, comprehend and navigate our way through. Confronted
with situations beyond our control, we instinctively seek refuge in
coping strategies of our own creation – ingenious mechanisms
crafted from our raw, unfiltered emotions and experiences.

Think back to your own childhood. Recall the moments when
life felt overwhelming, when big and difficult feelings threatened
to engulf you. In those moments, you crafted coping strategies –
be they retreating into a world of imagination, seeking solace in
familiar routines, or donning a mask of bravado to shield yourself
from vulnerability.

These coping strategies are not random twists of fate, they are the result of our innate resilience and resourcefulness. They serve as our armour, our shield against the onslaught of uncertainty and adversity. But as we journey through life, they can also become our shackles, trapping us in patterns that no longer serve our highest good.

Sometimes pain feels easier than the truth

When I am rooted in my authentic nature, I know that doing life with others is good for me. That being among community feels natural, uplifting and true for me. That opening my heart, trusting others and being vulnerable is right for me. In my authentic nature, I know that taking a seat inside my selfhood is good. That being real and honest with who I am and where I'm at in life feels true. That celebrating others as they are, and me as I am, is right.

So why do I have an egoic orientation towards individualism? What did I take in, absorb, experience and give meaning to, and how did that send me on a venture far far away from the real me?

One night, when my parents were both out, my Aunty Julie rang to check in on my brother and me (once again, my guardian angel!). I answered the phone and she could tell immediately that something wasn't right. She was spot on. I'd been walking around the house with a knife in my hand and rubbing the blade against my wrist. I had no real intention of taking my own life, but the thoughts in my head had certainly considered that a lot. It had been happening since Grade 6 when a so-called friend had said to me, 'Go home and kill yourself, no one will care anyway!' I thought, *Well, if they think that, maybe I should.* From there I developed an ongoing narrative of not deserving to be alive, not deserving to be here, not deserving to take up space.

Although I hadn't said anything to Aunty Julie, her instincts told her to come over. I answered the front door wrapped in a towel, clearly not in a good way. Aunty Julie could see something was wrong and asked what it was. I showed her my wrist. Dad was at work and wasn't going to be home until late. I'm not sure where Mum was. I didn't want Aunty Julie to tell Dad what I'd done. She often stood up for us and listened to what we needed, but this time she said it was too serious not to tell Dad. *Fuck, it's all coming out!* Aunty Julie called Dad and asked him to come home early, which he did.

When he got home, she met him at the door and told him I had been doing something very disturbing. We all sat down in my parents' bedroom at the foot of the bed. I was fidgeting and outrageously nervous. It was like we were sitting in a pit of awkwardness which I had to pierce with my words. There was so much to say but it was all jammed up in my throat and it felt like someone had pressed the mute button on me. The words wanted to come out but it was like I had no voice. I was desperate to get it out perfectly and have Dad hold me tenderly. But I'd felt so much shame for so long, I couldn't trust that others wouldn't feel the same way about me.

I started by saying that I cut myself because my brother Matt had called me fat (sorry, Matt). Neither Dad nor Aunty Julie bought it – and honestly, I knew they wouldn't. *Come on, Kat, get to the truth of it, would you. Why is it so damn hard?* I had the stage, the meta-phorical mic, people who loved me in front of me. *Just start talking!*

'Something happened to me when I was six years old . . .'

Coping mechanisms on steroids

Many of the coping mechanisms I developed were me trying to control a world that seemed chaotic and wildly unsafe. Those mechanisms were directed inwards, and were obviously harmful, but other personas and behavioural strategies can appear, at least externally, as the traits of successful people. Again, take a look at the Enneagram work to see how one's coping strategies intensify when our level of self-awareness diminish.

Do you know anyone who is highly successful in their career – who seems to be always available for their colleagues and clients, receives regular praise from their boss and co-workers, is always first in line to get a promotion or pay rise, has the house, car and wardrobe – all the outward trappings of success? Some might call this successful, but these behaviours are red flags indicating Enneagram #3 The Achiever, someone who's working their absolute ring off to prevent themselves from failing. They cope by never sitting still to compensate for their fear of being a failure.

Such behaviours were clearly apparent in my client Jane's husband. His behaviour not only affected him, but his friends and family too. Jane said to me one day, 'I wish my husband would sit next to me on the couch and hold my hand. But he mows the lawn, whipper snips the sidewalk to perfection, fiddles in the garage, blows the leaves and picks up the leaves, changes all the light globes and more. I know where this comes from and it's not healthy for him. I just want to hold his hand!'

How about the sympathetic friend – the one who is always there with a shoulder to cry on, who organises the food roster when someone is sick, attends every fundraiser, will take a call at

midnight, says 'yes' to any request? I wonder if they ever find them-
selves too exhausted to go on, but too terrified of saying no, in
case no one likes them anymore. They cope by being everything
to everyone as they feel unworthy and are desperate to be known
and seen as a 'good person'.

And what about the friend who is constantly sick, or tired, has
just been dumped, whose cat has just died, has a rash, earache,
headache, sprained ankle, sick grandmother, got broken into,
got scammed – all of which are legitimate, but gosh, it makes you
wonder how one person can attract so much 'bad luck'?

What is your default coping mechanism?

Remember how I used to OCD the shit out of my bedroom when
I was fourteen? I've carried this coping strategy to this very day.
When life gets a bit tight, overwhelming or suffocating, the first
thing I do is clean. I'm talking wash-the-walls clean. Vacuum-outside
clean. Wash-every-bit-of-clothing clean. Pick-up-every-strand-of-
invisible-dust-on-the-floor clean. At the root of this compulsion is
my sense of control, or lack thereof.

It's embarrassing (to my ego) to admit that I still use this
coping strategy but, thankfully, it's not as consuming as it once
was. At one point, when I lived with my brother in my twenties,
I was vacuuming and mopping the house *four times a day*. How
relaxing it was to live with me! Another go-to strategy around that
time was to turn on my sad-sap story about my past when my boy-
friend was going out, so he'd stay home with me. I couldn't deal
with being alone with myself so I would reach for the first thing I
thought would keep him at home. He caught onto it after a while
and learnt to leave, regardless of my pity-party attempts.

What other coping strategies might we activate when we are feeling out of control?

Manipulation. This involves subtly influencing or controlling others' thoughts, feelings, or actions to serve your own agenda, often through tactics like guilt-tripping, gaslighting, or emotional manipulation.

Micromanagement. The ego may seek to maintain a sense of control by excessively monitoring and interfering with the activities and decisions of others, often driven by a fear of failure or a need for perfection.

Domination. In situations where the ego feels threatened or insecure, it may resort to dominating others through assertive or aggressive behaviour, seeking to establish power and superiority over them.

Defensiveness. When the ego feels challenged or criticised, it may instinctively respond with defensiveness, seeking to protect itself from perceived threats to its identity or self-worth.

Comparison and competition. The ego often thrives on comparisons with others, seeking to assert its superiority or maintain a (false) sense of self-worth through competition and comparison, even at the expense of others' wellbeing.

Approval-seeking. The ego may become overly concerned with seeking validation and approval from others, shaping our behaviour and decisions to meet external expectations rather than aligning with our authentic self.

Perfectionism. Driven by a fear of failure or inadequacy, the ego may strive for perfection in all aspects of life, imposing unrealistic standards on us and others and experiencing distress when these standards are not met.

Attachment to outcomes. The ego often becomes fixated on specific outcomes or results, attaching our sense of self-worth and happiness to external achievements or circumstances, leading to frustration and disappointment when expectations are not met.

Avoidance and escapism. In response to discomfort or uncertainty, the ego may resort to avoidance or escapism, seeking to distract us from difficult emotions or situations rather than confronting them directly.

Dependency. The ego may develop a dependency on external factors or individuals for validation, security, or happiness, relinquishing its own agency and autonomy in the process.

These control dynamics serve to reinforce the ego's sense of identity and security. Recognising and addressing these patterns is essential for greater self-awareness and fostering authentic growth and fulfillment.

Get this tool into your life: Assess Your Stress

Let's not play the avoidance game. Instead, let's get real and honest about what is creating stress and unease in your life. Remember, these stressors add up and take you deeper into your default coping strategies which in turn take you further from your true nature. Which of these areas in your life are activating your default coping mechanisms?

Is it money? Do you stress about money? Do you resist looking at your bank account, how much you spend or make or owe because you 'just can't deal?' How are you currently 'coping' in ways that don't serve you?

Is it your relationship? Do you worry that you're losing intimacy and connection? Do you wonder if you're in the right relationship but fear that there's no one else out there? Do you want to say something but are too scared that it'll open a Pandora's box of, 'Yeah, I'm unhappy, I think we should break up'? How are you currently 'coping' with that in ways that don't serve you?

Is it your health and wellbeing? Do you want to eat better but can't seem to 'stick to it'? Do you sign up for exercise classes but never go because you feel 'yuck'? How are you currently 'coping' with that in ways that don't serve you?

Is it your past? Do you run from your past, skim over it, or have you blacked out your childhood? Do you get tsunami-sized waves of emotions when you see someone in a movie or real life get over-powered? How are you currently 'coping' with that in ways that don't serve you?

Is it your work? Do you feel your time's up with where you're at but worry you don't know your next move? Do you dream about creating your own venture or changing your career path altogether, but fear it'll be the wrong move? How are you currently 'coping' with that in ways that don't serve you?

I share these examples as I have lived these scenarios and many more. At those times, I wanted to do something about them but stood frozen with fear, doubt, concern, worry, overwhelm and stress, all the while knowing that staying stuck was doing jack-fucking-shit to change anything. As I've mentioned, being real and honest with yourself is a hard and gigantic pill to swallow. It leads you to the truth, the root, the answer. It leads you to freedom.

Meet Effie

In my coaching program on a live call, my client Effie shared her story. She had recently overcome breast cancer, which included a bilateral mastectomy and reconstruction. Shortly afterwards, her fiancé had left her without a word, letter, text message, voice byte or conversation.

Her coping strategy was to 'see the light', 'get the lesson', 'learn from the pain' – which is absolutely bang on. Except that, in practice, that meant Effie allowed very little space for letting her deep pain and anger be heard and felt. Instead of processing her pain, she jumped straight 'to the light, to the love' because it made her, temporarily, feel better.

Now, this might sound like a nice approach, but when we dug deeper, Effie shared that when she was a little girl, her parents split up. Her world, once safe, instantly crumbled. Her parents became so consumed in their hate for one another, that she practically had to raise herself.

'Being the eldest child, I always felt dutiful in taking care of everyone other than myself. The Greek tradition of serving everyone else's needs before your own was strong in our family. Running yourself into the ground for your family was a badge of honour!'

Along the way, Effie had taught herself to 'get on with it', another coping strategy, all the while feeling abandoned by her parents and that she hadn't been enough for them to give her the love that she'd needed. Over time, she developed more coping strategies, like doing life alone, overstretching herself and making herself overly available for others, in the hope that these strategies would show that she was 'enough' to be loved.

'The stories and scars I carried from a young age were that I was never good enough. My parents expected a lot and I always felt like I fell short or could have tried harder and done better. I became good at being an empath, intuitively reading people's emotions – I had to, so I could keep everyone happy (but myself).'

We used the Ego Clearing tool (described in Chapter 13) to help her get into the ick and fully examine the 'Oh Kat, I don't want to go there' schtick. Tough titties, we're going there. In facing her pain head-on, Effie unearthed the meaning she was giving to the real-life pain of her fiancé leaving her. The story she created was that she is not loveable as she is, using her post-cancer reality as its support pillar. *Who will love this body? I'm a shell of my former self. I have to get back to the old Effie. I'm back to raising myself again, just like when I was little. I did everything right and he still left me!*

Effie's ego was about to send her on yet another quest to 'better herself'. I stopped her and posed this question, 'What is the *true* focus here, Effie? Where would your time, energy and life force be better placed?' Effie couldn't answer this, so she asked for guidance. 'Would you like to get to know the Effie that stands in front of you right now and love her a little more each day?' I asked. 'Would you like to leave the old Effie behind, knowing she's had her time? Would you like to reclaim the you standing before you? To learn to love her – to love yourself – as you are?'

Effie held her heart and cried.

Bonus tool: Little You Chats

A tool I call Little You Chats is really useful in cases like Effie's. She was a woman operating as a wounded child seeking to be loved. The wounded child in her thought, *The more I can be, the more I can do, the more I can offer, then I'll be loved. Then I'll belong.* What Effie needed was to love the little girl in her *as she is,* which in turn will help her love the woman she is.

Each time I use this exercise with my clients, they heal the hurt of their inner child. Over time the pain subsides, allowing them to become more present in their adult lives and relationships. These are the steps I take my clients through to help them get in touch with their inner child and integrate them into their adult experience, with love.

Locate in your body where there is pain, unease, tension, tightness or whatever uncomfortable feeling there might be.

Place your hands over that area of your body, close your eyes and acknowledge that there is a part of you that feels your emotion.

Ask, 'Which little [your name] is here in this moment?' Generally an image or a feeling of oneself at a particular age and stage arises with that prompt.

Ask, 'What do you want to say and share with me? I am here, I am listening.' Reassure them that you have heard what they said and felt. Imagine holding them and comforting them and telling them that they are now safe and okay. Make sure they feel seen and validated in a way that they were not at the time.

Ask, 'How are you feeling now? Are you good? Are you safe?'

For as long as your younger self needs, hold them in a loving embrace. Then, when they and you are ready, put your little self somewhere safe inside you as you continue to move throughout your day.

Check in at regular intervals, remind them that they are safe, that you've got them and that you're comfortably in control of where you're both headed now in life. Because they are always watching and wondering, will I be okay?

Using this tool helps us reset the story our ego has built around a situation and lay a new foundation for our future. The reality of what happened is one thing. The meaning we give it takes it to a whole new level and builds the ego's force field, shaping how you view yourself, others and the world.

I know I keep banging on about it but understanding how this works is *so* important! If we want a greater life than the one we're living now, it's our personal responsibility to try to discern our stressors, catch our habituated responses to them and question where and how we need to change. You can't always change your situation, but you can absolutely change how you navigate it.

Chapter 5

The wake-up call

We forget to remember

Why is it that we venture away from ourselves? Why do we 'forget' what is right, good and true for us? Why do we forgo our intuitive sense and rely on the big ball of thoughts between our ears to help us make it through life? No one comes into this world and consciously thinks, *Yeah, what a great idea! I am going to consciously forget who I am, what I'm about, what is right, good and true for me and live a life that has nothing to do with what is of deep importance to me. Oh, and while I'm at it, I'll venture incredibly far away from my authentic nature and become who I think the world wants me to be.* No one!

So why do we forget our inherent knowing of who we are? Why do we go about our lives living in such a way that isn't right, good and true for us? Why do we doubt our own sense of knowing and disregard the matters that matter?

Since the age of twenty-four, I've been on a quest to discover, uncover and recover more of Kat. The real Kat. Not the, 'I'll act like an air-head Kat, so you think I'm easygoing and like me more!' Not the, 'I'll say yes from my head Kat, even though my body is screaming a giant FUCK NO, I don't want to have sex with you!' Not the, 'I'll pretend that I don't need you Kat, even though I so want to be loved and share how I really feel!' I've had so many iterations of 'who shall I be today' that it exhausts me just thinking about it. I'm a recovering chameleon and have been in remission for some time now.

As I went on my quest, I embarked upon a Graduate Diploma of Psychology, sat in rooms listening to teachings from Deepak Chopra and Dr Wayne Dyer (my spirit guide), took myself through a myriad of personal development courses, meditation certification and more. Through all this, a common thread came about as to why we are the way we are, and why we end up where we are. Noted, the theories I learned may have differed slightly, but the foundations were the same.

Waking up to myself in that ice-cold bath and realising something drastic had to change was the beginning of unravelling and untangling myself from the ego; of calling in all my past selves in order to love, accept and guide them on a new path; of claiming my truth – all sides of it – the good, the bad, the cringe and the ugly.

Facing the truth hurts like hell

Dad, Aunty Julie and I were sitting at the foot of my parents' bed. 'What is it, Neng?' my dad asked. I could see in his eyes that he was terrified, but wanted to be strong for me. 'You can tell us anything.'

'Do you remember that family from church?' I mumbled. 'The ones we used to go on holidays with?'

Dad nodded. He looked over at Aunty Julie, concerned.

He and Mum and the other girls' parents would often go out together, leaving their second eldest daughter, who was around sixteen at the time, to babysit. Once the adults were out, or even sometimes while they were at home but distracted, this girl would take me into her room, undress me and dress me, like I was a doll. In my head I went along with it, but in my body it didn't feel right. At church she picked me up from underneath my dress and I knew it didn't feel right. I was about five. One summer, our families went away together. The parents went out to dinner, leaving us kids at home. My brother Matt was nine, I was six.

I was in my room alone. The windows were open and I remember the curtains moving slowly in the breeze. Everything was white, peaceful and serene – and then my door opened. Peeking out of one eye, I saw our babysitter walk in, dressed in a bath robe. The door closed and she took off her robe. She was naked. I remember thinking, *What is she doing?*

Keeping that one eye just open enough to see what was happening, but closed enough to look like I was asleep, I held my breath as she walked over and got into my bed. She started kissing me. She put her hands inside me and forced me to put my hands inside her. I don't remember how long this went on for, I just remember telling myself over and over, *Pretend you're asleep, pretend you're asleep, pretend you're asleep.* That was how I coped.

I was paralysed with fear. I couldn't move, but I could hear my head screaming. I don't know how long the assault lasted. I don't know when the girl left. I don't know how it ended. I don't know what happened afterwards. I don't know if she said anything. After that, I think my brain wanted me to forget, to block it out. To erase it. To let it melt into the endless abyss of subconscious repression. But it never stays there, does it?

That six-year-old little girl experienced something no one should. She made one person's wrongdoing mean everything about her sweet little self. It made her feel that she had to do life alone because no one is there for you. That it was okay for people to use her for their benefit and that the only way to stay safe was to go along with it. That she was not safe with the people she was meant to be safe with. That she must have been a very bad little girl for something like that to have happened. That she was dirty, filthy, tarnished, impure. That no one could ever love her, for she was damaged goods.

Oh Neng, little Neng, what a burden to carry so young. What weight and heaviness you must carry in your sweet little heart. Lighten your load, darling, put that baggage down, for none of it, not a bit of it, is true. Put the baggage down. Take it out of your heart and wherever else you have stored it and lay it down. Go play, be free, be a child of the earth and stars. You are loved. I love you. I love you. I love you.

I'd love to say that in that moment, acknowledging the truth of what had happened to me out loud to my closest family fixed everything. It didn't. At least, not straight away. It would be another eight years until my breakdown in the bath, and another four long years after that, for my body to work through and release all the pain it had built up and held in for so long. But it was the beginning. The beginning of reclaiming my truth and my whole self, piece by piece, word by word. The start of my journey back home and living as my authentic self.

Authenticity is an inside job

At the root of it, authenticity is our willingness to be real and honest with ourselves, first and foremost, so we can show up real and honest in our lives. Let that one sink in. To be real and honest with ourself, the person looking back in the mirror, the person you're inside of each and every day, the person you wake up in, eat breakfast, lunch and dinner in, the person you go to work in, go on dates in, shower, shit and then go to bed in.

We're pretty good at fooling ourselves, selling ourselves sophisticated stories, thinking that they are our truth, and warping reality as a result. So it may take a while before being real and honest with ourselves, our relationship to others, money, wellbeing, purpose, contribution, and all the rest starts to feel comfortable. Stick with it – it may take a few hundred rounds of shoving that realness down in the hope it'll never be found before that honesty starts to feel good. And when it does, you'll realise that doing the work has been so, so worth it.

To be aligned with our authentic nature is to come back home to what feels right for us, good for us and true for us. Because when we are in tune with that, we are living in accordance with our personal and unique values, we are listening to the wise voice within, tapped into our intuition, our senses, our body. We hear the calls of what we need, crave and yearn for, and we darn well do something about it. We are present with our essence, and that's it, right there. When we live and breathe from this place, authenticity becomes a force field that is palpable, strengthened by every move we make.

Authenticity is an *inside job*, there's no escaping that – try all you might to copy another or avoid this path. Ignoring the work that's in front and ahead of you to bypass all the shit, all the mud and all the gunk you gotta face, make peace with, love, befriend and surrender, is tempting, believe me it's tempting, but it will take you *further away* from yourself. And the question you want to ask yourself is, *Am I okay with that?*

Gnarly wake-up calls

In my previous life as a registered nurse, my graduate year placement was at The Alfred Hospital in Cardiothoracics. We'd care for patients who had just come out of cardiac bypass surgery and it was a full-on recovery. There was constant monitoring in the first twenty-four to seventy-two hours post-surgery. The patients were pretty out of it while we drew blood, checked drains and kept an eye on their test results. Many were men in their late forties to sixties. As I cared for them, I took the time to sit with them, get to know them, ask how they were *really* going. Many of them shared a common story.

They'd done the 'right thing'. Worked hard, provided for their family, paid down the mortgage. They lived stressful, busy lives without thinking much about what they really wanted. 'I mean, sure, I would've loved to have been at home more with my wife, spent more time with my children, but you can't do that.' Having the heart attack encouraged them to re-evaluate their lives. Their heart attack and the surgery made them stop, slow down and reassess the burger with the lot. By day four post-surgery, most of them had a breakdown moment. A realisation.

Sometimes, we need something pretty gnarly to wake us up, to shake us into our senses and snap us out of doing what we've always done. For the patients I met at The Alfred, this was their 'something gnarly'. For my client Tina, it was the realisation that no matter how hard she tried to portray perfection, every time she walked through her front door, a great big emotional mess (not a literal one) was right there waiting for her. For my client Katrina, it was her husband cheating on her while she was trying to be everything to their children and give more than what she had left in the tank to her work. For me, my something gnarly was being so high on drugs I couldn't recognise myself, and being forced to admit my truth about sexual abuse, brain surgery and chronic pain.

In truth, we are forever being 'woken up' and being called to deeper layers of authenticity as we move through our lives. We might lose ourselves in a new relationship, in a new work venture, in a new friendship group, in becoming a parent or bonus parent, in a divorce, in losing a loved one, in ill health. As you resurface from the depths of losing yourself, there will be a moment where you long to 'find you' again. I've said it before, and I'll keep saying it: being our authentic selves is not a one-time thing that's over and done with. It's a forever thing.

Get this tool into your life: Your Something Gnarly

What's the something gnarly trying to wake you up? Get real and honest and notice it. Do you want to continue having to face the weight of 'something gnarly' to shake you awake, or are you ready and willing to do the work and address your obstacles before they reach the weight of the gnarly wake-up call?

- Is it constant back pain, now at a point where you can barely walk?
- Is it constant money issues, now at a point where you can't pay rent?
- Is it constant alcohol use, now at a point where you black out and can't remember parts of the night?
- Is it constant self-loathing and pity, now at a point where your partner leaves?
- Is it constant anxiety, now at a point where you think it's heart palpitations and go to hospital, but it's not your heart?

Meet Lynn

Being real and honest sits alongside being the observer, getting quiet so we can enquire after and listen to our core values. There's a level of willingness needed to face the truth because we know that once we see it, hear it or feel it, it's really fricken hard to unsee, unhear or unfeel it. The clients who work with me have this willingness, even though they are shit scared, because they want a new way forward. They need a new way forward. It's no longer an, 'Oh yeah, that'll be nice.' It becomes, 'It's a must, Kat.' Once a client reaches this point they want to live, breathe and be authentically them. They're so done with the 'fake them' that, despite all the upheaval they know it might bring, they welcome being real and honest.

My client Lynn, a bloody legend might I add, was living in her Enneagram #3 The Achiever. She was busy being busy, fulfilling the 'get shit done' memo and working herself to sickness. Being ill was the only time she let herself rest, as when she was sick she had a 'reason' to call in sick.

Lynn works in real estate, manages two businesses with her husband, Larry, and she took over her dad's ship fuelling and bunkering business when he passed. In the last year she also became an empty nester. Upon reaching this significant life stage, she realised she'd spent her whole life doing things for everybody else (from her Achiever persona). She'd never been allowed to rest growing up – there'd always been 'something to do' around the house. The only way Lynn got any kind of reprieve from her parents was when she would run away for an entire day (her coping strategy) and not come back until dinner time.

She was always asked to 'Bake this, make that, get this on my desk by . . .' because people knew she'd get it done. Her ego thrived on getting shit done because it strengthened her identity as a doer, a go-getter, the human-doing Terminator. In saying 'yes' to everybody else, Lynn never asked herself what she wanted. Like, ever. She knew what her kids wanted, what her clients wanted, what her dad wanted, what her mum wanted. Everything was humming and getting done on the outside, but she was desperately wanting fulfillment on the inside.

She said, 'Kat, I'm in my fifties. I need her, I want her, I gotta have her in my life! I got to live for me!' By 'her', she meant her authentic self. The *real* Lynn. In one of our sessions, I asked her to be real and honest with me about the areas of her life that she wanted to shift, even if she felt fear and angst about it. She said, 'I want to let go of my dad's business. I want to reduce my hours in real estate. I want to consolidate mine and Larry's businesses. I want to live at our farmhouse, create a beautiful garden, live off the land. I want to go slow. I want to sleep during the day if I need a sleep without worrying someone will find out. I want to watch a show without guilt. I want to simplify the hell out of my life.' I mean, yes Lynn, yes!

Lynn's willingness to be real and honest about not wanting to continue her dad's fuelling business meant she needed to have a hard chat with her mum – a mum she had worked very hard to please, keep happy and off her back for almost fifty years. Lynn's willingness to be real and honest by dropping her real-estate hours meant she needed to look at her finances to ensure this was possible, and then train someone to help her with the load. Lynn's willingness to be real and honest about wanting to go about her life more slowly, intently and in tune with herself meant she had some work to do with her ego and its stories. She had to deal with its resistance and learn new ways to manage and navigate its potency.

Being real and honest means you're willing to get very real with reality. When you do that, you see things more clearly. There's no warping of reality. Instead, you're faced *with* reality. The reality of your finances, the reality of the state of your relationships, the reality of your individual needs and wants, the reality of how you spend time, the reality of your wellbeing.

Generally, what follows is a feeling of overwhelm, of wanting to bury your head in the sand, re-blind yourself and block your ears to stunt your too-loud, newly felt sense of self. *The way it is* can be a lot. We realise how much we've fooled ourselves, tricked ourselves and convinced ourselves that all is fine. Or equally, convinced ourselves that all is terrible. This new awakening will make clear how aligned or misaligned you are with your authentic self. With that comes pain and questions as to *why* we did or didn't do *that*, behaved *this* or *that* way.

When Lynn and I were in one of our sessions, we used this model to visually see (A) where she is at right now, (B) where she wants to be and (C) what stories are in her way.

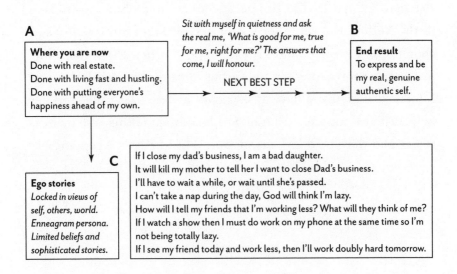

A

Where you are now
Done with real estate.
Done with living fast and hustling.
Done with putting everyone's happiness ahead of my own.

Sit with myself in quietness and ask the real me, 'What is good for me, true for me, right for me?' The answers that come, I will honour.

NEXT BEST STEP

B

End result
To express and be my real, genuine authentic self.

C

Ego stories
Locked in views of self, others, world. Enneagram persona. Limited beliefs and sophisticated stories.

If I close my dad's business, I am a bad daughter.
It will kill my mother to tell her I want to close Dad's business.
I'll have to wait a while, or wait until she's passed.
I can't take a nap during the day, God will think I'm lazy.
How will I tell my friends that I'm working less? What will they think of me?
If I watch a show then I must do work on my phone at the same time so I'm not being totally lazy.
If I see my friend today and work less, then I'll work doubly hard tomorrow.

In this visual example her life situation was clearly spelt out for her. Once we'd drawn it, she couldn't unsee it. Was she going to let the stories in her head derail her heart and authentic path? Was she going to discard the next best step of getting quiet with herself and asking for the first time in her life what she wanted? Not today, ego-Satan. Not today.

Lynn was ready to be real and honest in how she had made other people's desires her own. She knew it was time to live for her, no matter how awkward that might feel. She was ready to implement the next step, and let that step take her into new territory. From then, this has become her full-time practice. She now has journals filled with guidance. Lynn is well and truly on her true path. You bet she wakes up when her body says, *Okay, I'm ready!* You bet she takes it slow in the mornings with her coffee in bed, followed by a walk. You bet she doesn't start work until 10 am and never answers the phone before then. You bet she takes a nap in the middle of the day if her body calls for it. You bet she left the New Year's Eve party at a time that felt good for her, went home, watched *Sex and the City* in bed and woke up feeling fan-fricken-tastic. And all the while she's kept her husband informed of her changes, her growth, and he has supported her, the whole time. She hasn't shoved it down his throat or said, 'I'm doing this and I don't care what you have to say about it'. She hasn't misused her new authentic ways against him. She let him know this path matters to her and that she'd love his support. His love. His acceptance.

PART TWO

OUR WAY
BACK HOME

Chapter 6

Presence and awareness

The light and the shadow

To be on the authenticity path we have to be able to sit in our truth, no matter how uncomfortable it may be. Authenticity isn't like taking a leisurely walk down 'Everything is Merry Lane'. It's not just about embracing the parts of ourselves that we love and admire. It's about owning *every* facet of our being – the light *and* the shadow. Even when we claim to be on the path to authenticity, there's often a sneaky little gremlin lurking in the shadows – fake-authenticity. It's the wolf in sheep's clothing, masquerading as the real deal while secretly clinging to old patterns and pretences.

So why does fake-authenticity rear its head, even when we're seeking to be our true selves? It all comes down to fear – fear of judgement, fear of rejection, fear of not measuring up. It's the voice in our heads screeching, *What will they think if they see the real me? Will I still be accepted? Will I still belong?*

But here's the truth we must face: authenticity *isn't* about seeking validation or fitting in. It's about grounding in, standing for and owning all parts of ourselves and being very okay with that, no matter how messy or imperfect it may be. It's about having the courage to stand in our own power, even when the world – or our ego – tries to tear us down.

Revisiting your roots

Not long after my wake-up call in the bath, Mum asked if I'd like to join her on her annual trip to the Philippines. Little did I know that my parents had been chatting about how they were going to get me 'back on track'. They were worried and were struggling to handle my 'go fuck yourself' energy. The more they cared and gently asked about what I was up to, the more I pushed them away. Years later we spoke about this period and they admitted that they had been at their wits' end. They didn't want to lose me to drugs or the wrong boyfriend so they stopped asking after me, scared their questions would push me away altogether.

Looking back, I felt that distance between us. They'd stopped hounding me and asking their usual million questions (or what felt like a million questions). I wondered why. *Had I done something wrong? Did they not care about me?* In pushing so hard to gain the space to 'do my thing' and escape the feeling of being suffocated, I'd ended up feeling completely alone.

I went with Mum to the Philippines, not knowing just how badly I needed to go until I got there. I'd been plenty of times when I was younger. As my brother and I had grown up in Australia with all our physical needs met, my parents felt that taking us to the Philippines would not only keep us in touch with family, but also ground us and allow us to remember our family's humble beginnings, aka not be spoilt turds.

Whenever we stayed with our *Amang* and *Inang*, we lived simply. We showered with one bucket of cold water tipped over our heads.

We washed our clothes at the tap outside. Family members would climb the trees out the back and bring down bananas, coconuts and mangoes. We sat around, ate food, talked, and welcomed people who dropped by the house. I'd done this each time we returned to the Philippines, but this time, I noticed much more.

The kindness and genuine nature that people exuded forced me to question where such deep peace came from, especially when they had nothing, or what I deemed to be nothing. They could just sit around all day, talk to each other, have their feet up, and run their small shops that people would barely buy anything from – yet they were still happy, kind and welcoming. On that trip, Mum took me out with her old school friends. We sang karaoke, rode bikes and jeepneys, went to the markets and ate. We laughed, ate more and slept.

I remember *Amang* and *Inang* sitting on their red swing on the balcony, watching people go by. They'd swing, they'd talk, they'd swing, they'd say hello to people, they'd swing some more. There was such simplicity in their way of being. I, on the other hand, had loads of *things* they didn't have, and I wasn't happy or at peace. Even in my self-absorbed state, I could see that they had what I didn't – contentment. Inner peace. Deep fulfillment. What I now know as spiritual richness, though, had you asked me what to call it back then, I wouldn't have had a clue.

When I returned to Australia, nothing much had changed. It was summer festival season and my friends were all in, but something inside of me just couldn't bring myself to go. The thought of it made me feel sick. A new and unrecognisable part of me felt like I would be disrespecting my culture, my roots. What I had learnt in the Philippines about contentment, kindness and peace had stuck, and I couldn't unstick it. I couldn't unfeel it. It felt wrong to get back into partying and abusing drugs. I was more surprised than my friends. I slowly tapered off the drugs without even trying to or forcing the matter. My body was saying 'no', and I was listening. Finally.

Something was changing. I didn't will for it to change. I didn't even really ask for it to change, well, at least not consciously. Something was being done to and for me from the inside, and although it was new territory, it felt familiar, like home.

Weaponising authenticity

There's something I see when it comes to authenticity that isn't so authentic. It's the ego disguising itself as authenticity, driving toxic behaviours of carelessness, separation, cocky confidence and entitlement. Let me explain.

I see people weaponising authenticity, using it against others as a way to excuse their behaviour and give themselves free rein to say and do what they want. They think, *Hey, if you don't like it, then that's your problem.* While there are elements of truth to that, I'm talking here about the defensive nature and tone with which people use authenticity as a shield to excuse shitty behaviour.

I see people acting and behaving with a false, cocky confidence and a reckless bravado. This is the ego disguising itself as authenticity and warping the mind into thinking that they have every right to say or do whatever they want to do because they are being 'true to themselves'. This is *not* authenticity. This is the ego looking for power and control to excuse itself from how actions have ramifications. If that's you, please stop.

Being authentic is not about having free rein to say or do whatever you want without care or thought of how this might affect someone else. This is where people often get confused. They think that in order to be true to themselves, they must say everything on their mind and do everything that feels right regardless of how others might feel. True authenticity comes with true responsibility. I know this because I too went through this stage. In fact, it is very common when you're on the journey towards your authentic self. Being separate from your authentic nature for a long time and then reacquainting yourself with it is not just a matter of going from zero to hero in ten seconds! It's a long-arse journey. Along that journey you may well find yourself misusing the power of authenticity.

The pain of inauthentic authenticity

When I went through this stage, all I wanted to do was whatever the hell I wanted to do! I had blinkers on as to how others might feel. I missed birthday parties, engagements, weddings, dinners and much more because I simply didn't feel like going. In my mind, I was honouring what *I* wanted and that helped me sleep at night. But after doing my thing for a while, the invitations stopped coming. My phone didn't ring or ping as much as it used to, and I felt lonely. I swung from Little Miss People Pleaser to Little Miss Independent. The irony was I felt lonely in *both* those states.

As the people pleaser, I felt lonely because I didn't know myself. I missed connection to myself. As the fierce independent, I felt lonely because I shut the world out. I missed connection with others. This swing between states is very common and is referred to as 'overcompensating'. For all the years I people-pleased and didn't honour myself, I made up for it by doing only the things that would serve myself. In trying to pay back for what I missed, I took it too close to the edge.

Is this bad? No. Is this wrong? No. Is this normal? Yes. It's something to watch out for, to notice. As you navigate back to your authentic nature, you will venture into places you haven't been for some time. The outside world might see it as a selfish phase, an outspoken phase, a hibernation phase, or an overly expressive phase. And you know what, that might be the phase you experience and that's okay. What you want to do, ultimately, is become aware and notice how this phase feels for you *and* how it affects others. You want to ask yourself if you're truly okay with that.

One of my friends texted to tell me how disappointed she was that I bailed on attending her birthday at the last minute. I remember driving home from work, thinking about going to her party and just not feeling it. So I texted to say that I wasn't feeling so good and that I'd make it up to her. That night, her partner proposed and it turned into an engagement party. When I found out, I felt a deep pang in my guts. It wasn't guilt. It was, *Fuck, I would've loved to have been there for her and to have witnessed that.* I didn't hear from her for weeks, even though I sent many texts to say congratulations. The people pleaser in me awoke again and wanted to do everything possible for her not to be mad. Then I shifted gears into Little Miss I Don't Give A Fuck, telling myself that I'd done what felt right for me in that moment and if she couldn't accept that, then she wasn't my real friend. This is Defence 101.

I learnt a lot from that moment. The phase of doing what I wanted had felt good, but the way I went about it, careless of how it might affect others, didn't. My friend sent me a text explaining how she saw our friendship, what she wanted from friendships and that she thought it would be best to have some space. That hurt. It hurt because I knew it didn't need to be that way and that I needed to take responsibility for how my 'being true to me' might not have been so pure after all. That maybe, just maybe, my ego had gotten hold of me, disguised itself as authenticity and tricked me into believing that *this* is what authentic living is.

This is what I learnt. Authentic living *isn't* about shutting people out and making them the problem. Nor is it about having your nose shoved so far up someone's butt for their approval. There's a space between these two states of operating that we can experience. If you're seeking true, grounded and responsible authenticity, then you *have* to find that space in between.

While I'm on this thought train, I also want to clear something up that I believe is really important. *People* aren't inauthentic, it's their *behaviour* that's inauthentic. The truth of a person, their authentic nature, resides beneath the persona, the ego tactics, the patterned responses and behaviours. When we think someone's inauthentic, what we are seeing on the outside is a person whose ego is in the driver's seat, hijacking their view of self, others and the world and calling the shots in accordance with their limited belief system. They are being told who and how they have to be in order to feel capable, powerful, in control, safe, accepted, worthy, enough or perfect. At the deepest level, *this is not who they are,* therefore it is not *them* who's being inauthentic. It's the *persona* that is being inauthentic.

You'll see it on social media where people post stories of themselves pouting from every possible chin and jaw angle they can find. They're posing for photos like they're posing for a *Vogue* photoshoot, gazing at the sky, frolicking among the trees, placing their feet, shoulder angles and their 'good side' in front of the camera. They appear to ooze confidence. But when you meet them in real life, they're shy, guarded, self-conscious and have closed-down energy. They give off a certain persona for the screen, then when you meet them, it doesn't match up.

This is an important distinction for us to remember when judging others for being inauthentic, or even calling ourselves inauthentic. The next time that thought comes into your head or if you're about to say those words aloud, pause and remember this truth, because when you do, greater acceptance and compassion is available to you.

Get this tool into your life: Be the Observer

As we observe our behaviours, we are then invited to look more deeply. This part is, of course, up to you.

I get that going inward is bound to rattle and disturb old ways of thinking, doing and being, and that it will have you questioning how you once viewed the world. But that's the whole point, is it not? We are in a forever dance edging closer to our next layer of evolution and as this happens, we gotta dive deeper.

Let's practise

What situation is knocking on your door, where, if you invited your observer self to reflect, it would see what's really going on? What situation is inviting you into the work?

When we notice a tug-of-war moment with what we know to be right, good and true for us versus how we are currently responding, the invitation that's being slid under your door says:

> *DEAR YOU, IT'S TIME TO GET QUIET, ENQUIRE & LISTEN.*
>> *TIME: Now (or very soon).*
>> *LOCATION: Somewhere you won't be disturbed.*
>> *RSVP: You're already doing this, there's no getting out of it.*

This is where you take a question, pose it to the wise, intuitive being within (yes, you are one), be open and willing to receive guidance and information that will expand you beyond your current ways, and listen. Your ego is going to resist. Your ego will say things like, *This is a waste of time, you'll never get the answer, you don't have an intuitive wise voice or being inside; it doesn't matter, who cares!*

Then, when you receive an answer, the stories will fire up again. *How do you know this is right? How do you know this is the answer? How do you know this came from your intuitive wise being? What if it's the wrong answer?*

Please remember, your ego is doing what it knows best which is to keep you bound to its locked-in views of yourself. Expanding beyond the ego is its absolute worst nightmare and it'll say just about anything to keep you in what it knows.

This is when you must trust in your body. When you receive an answer, you'll feel an all-knowing in your physical being, a drop in your shoulders, a relaxation at your centre. It may take a few goes until you notice the difference between your ego voice and voice of truth. But it'll happen.

Meet Emma

I went to see Kat originally because I was scared – I'd had an intense episode of anxiety and depression and was worried about it happening again. I wanted to see someone who could support me with tools to get through another potential episode, so my life wouldn't crumble.

I contacted Kat to ask for recommendations for a psychiatrist with a holistic approach. But the moment I spoke to Kat, I felt this rush of energy through the phone and I knew that she was who I needed to see.

What I got was literally life changing. One of the first things Kat said to me was something like, 'You know, I've always thought you're too creative to be working in that big, dry corporation you work at.'

Over the next few months Kat worked with me to tease out what my heart truly wanted in life. She taught me to get to know my ego and how it can get in the way of us achieving what we really want. She also gave me tools to work on manifesting my life choices each day.

I had a lot of resistance to Kat's original comment but halfway through the coaching, the stars aligned and I got inspiration to start taking my passion in music more seriously. I started a music composition short course and asked my work if I could go down to four days so I could focus the other day on creating and learning about music. Work agreed and I'm currently a month into the new agreement. I've gone from having written just two songs (before seeing Kat) to now having written nearly 30 songs. I'm collaborating with two producers to bring my song ideas to life. I'm learning guitar and have bought digital audio equipment to learn how to create the music I hear in my head.

Even though I'm just a beginner in music, I feel like I'm living my authentic self much more so than I have in the last 15 years of my corporate career. I haven't had another anxiety/depression episode and I wonder if it came about from not expressing who I really am. But if it does surface again, I feel like I'll be more equipped to deal with it thanks to the tools that Kat has shown me.

Emma wrote this in 2020 after we'd worked together for six months. Afterwards, she left her corporate job, produced one of her songs on Spotify, and now creates wealth through creative expressions, music included, and is living life as who she is. Emma had lived her life based on a belief that wasn't even hers, 'you can't make money in the arts'. (*This is why this work is so damn important.*) And, in time, she began to question this belief and instead ask one good question: 'Well, what if I could?'

Bonus tool: One Good Question

I said to Emma that when she noticed her self-sabotaging ego trying to drag her down, she had to stop it in its tracks with 'one good question'.

'What should that question be?' she asked me.

'Well,' I replied, 'it can be any good question, so long as it directly neutralises and silences the negative story running in your head.' At that point, I shared an example from my own practice.

When I do my guest speaking gigs, there'll be running commentary inside my head that goes a lot like, *Oooh, you better be funny, Kat, so they like you more! Oooh, you better be less 'you' and a little more put together so they won't think you're a nut bag! Oooh, you better look up some smart facts or quotes so they think you're intelligent! Oooh, you better be a bit serious because they look like a serious crowd!*

This commentary does its best to have me act in a 'safe' way, leaving no room for anything else. So before I step on stage, I ask myself one good question: *If I were equal to these people, how would I be? How would I speak? How would I show up?*

By including the word 'equal' in the question, I remind myself that the crowd is only human, just like me. That each person out there has fears, dreams, families, heartaches, yearnings, just like me. My answer to the question is always, *If I were equal, I'd show up relaxed and at ease. I'd speak from my heart and share human to human.* This diffuses and neutralises my ego story, bringing me back home. I embody 'Kat'.

Once Emma had nailed the art of asking one good question, she was on her way. Instead of, 'How can I get rid of this anxiety forever?', it was, 'What is this anxiety trying to tell me?' Instead of, 'You can't make money in the arts', it was, 'How many songs are inside of me busting to come out?' Instead of, 'What if I make the wrong move and leave corporate and it doesn't work out?', it was, 'What's possible when I live true to who I am?'

Chapter 7

Facing truths

It hurts, but it's worth it

Being the observer takes us beyond the ego to a place where we watch ourselves from the outside in. When we sense that what we're doing isn't aligned with our true nature, this is the moment to step outside of ourselves and observe our behaviour from a distance. Once we have that perspective, it's then time to go inside. We need to get quiet, enquire and listen to that part of us that holds a clearer perspective, that can give us the next piece of the puzzle to help us come back home.

This is the step too many of us are afraid to take: the step inwards, from head to heart, to the core, to the centre of truth. The core never lies, which is why we stay in the land of complaining, bitching, moaning, blaming, projecting, indecisioning and tennis-matching for a few more years, maybe even decades, because our egos are so very clever at fuelling the fire of fear. Fear of change, fear of the unknown, fear of anything other than who it says you are, have to be and must remain.

When you get quiet, enquire and listen, you find joy and vitality. In those moments, something far greater than your ego will communicate with you and through you. This is the difference between the ego and how the truth resonates in your body where it feels right for you, good for you, true for you, despite the stories.

Will the real Kat John please stand up

During my peak partying period, I was going out with a guy whose best friend was a drug dealer. The guy I was dating loved drugs and in the beginning of our relationship we took them together. I abandoned myself again and again. But when I returned from the Philippines, something had shifted. I was being pushed along a new path and though I had no idea where it was taking me, I knew I couldn't ignore it. This was a force of its own, which didn't so much speak to me in words, but through feelings and a deep knowing.

My boyfriend didn't have a car or much money. And the little money he had, he was a tight-arse with. He always relied on me to pick him up, drop him off and pay for things. Now, I don't mind helping someone out or taking it in turns paying for meals or movies, but he was taking the piss and I let him piss all over me. One afternoon, we were going to pick up drugs for him and stopped at a 7-Eleven on the way. Although I'd just returned from overseas, he didn't ask a single thing about my trip. He just lazed casually in the passenger seat and said, 'Babe, can I borrow some cash, please please please?'

Despite his seriously hot looks, suddenly this gorgeous specimen of a man appeared very ugly to me. My rose-coloured glasses weren't so rosy anymore and I finally saw how toxic our relationship was. I was always at his beck and call – asking him questions, caring about him, giving him money, driving him wherever he wanted to go. Why wasn't I giving him the 'fuck off' energy I'd been giving out in spades to my parents?

As we drove, Michael Jackson's 'Man in the Mirror' was playing on the radio. The lyrics seemed to emphasise the ideas that had surfaced following my trip. I couldn't stop thinking about changing my life for the better. I was wondering how I might contribute to making a difference in the world. At that time, I thought my chances were pretty slim because I was far more identified with my ego self, but the thought was there nonetheless. In that moment, something inside of me broke and I knew I couldn't continue in the relationship with the hot-not-hot guy. So I dug deep into my truth and got real and honest with myself *and* him. I told him I was done, that I couldn't continue in our relationship, that this wasn't going to work.

He looked at me and said, 'Are you fucking serious?'

I was.

This time, I was ready to say no with my behaviour and my being.

This time, I was ready to use my words to serve me.

This time, I was ready to honour my boundaries and stick to them, no matter how much flattery, batting of eyelids or nice words he used to try to make me stay.

This time, I was ready to do what felt right, good and true for me. The *proper kind* of right, good and true for me. For the real Kat. The one deep below all the pain and hurt and drug use and partying. The Kat that was connected to the source of life. *That* Kat.

This was my moment.

I was finally willing to be real and honest with myself, him and my life!

He asked me to drive him to a friend's house. As I dropped him off, we both did a casual, see-ya-later type goodbye. No emotion, no heartbreak. It was done – and *I* had done it. I had finally chosen to give up something that wasn't in my best interest. My drug taking and behaviour led my parents to give me space. My loneliness led to me going on a three-day bender. The three-day bender led to a breakdown. The breakdown led to me going back to my roots. My roots led me to my truth. My truth led me to make a powerful choice. That powerful choice reminded me of the feeling of self-love, self-respect and self-worth I'd felt when I was that bright little spark of a kid.

I cried after I dropped him off; tears of relief, tears of pride, tears of *Shit, this is what it feels like to honour and be me.* The woman in the mirror made a change for the good, for once in her life.

Owning your truth

Owning your truth is ongoing work. Though you may have break-through moments of recognition and realisation, it takes care, time and effort to reintegrate all the lost parts of your self.

For so long, I denied the truth about being sexually abused. First, I blinded myself. Then, when glimpses of it came through, I allowed my friends' awkward responses to shut it down. When I shared it with the school counsellor, I blamed myself. When I first told Dad and Aunty Julie, I pretended that I was 'okay'.

But denying the monster only fed it. Each time I pretended it didn't exist, it grew. And grew. And grew. So I kept developing worse and worse behaviours to deflect it, to keep my eyes from seeing, my ears from hearing and my heart from knowing. I took drugs to warp my mind so I would no longer have to listen to my thoughts. I became so removed from myself, I no longer recog-nised myself in the mirror. Until I broke.

Reconnecting with my roots allowed me to take the next best step back towards my true self. Though not ready to face her head-on, I could allow little pieces to resurface. When enough of me had risen, I reclaimed those parts of myself. I said no more to toxic relationships, no more to (some) shitty behaviours and no more to keeping the truth shoved inside. I thought I had broken free, but apparently, I was just getting warmed up.

Being yourself is an honour

When Steve and I first got together, he was a pizza-eating machine. When I'd go over to his place, he'd always be ordering pizza. In truth, I didn't want pizza but I acted all cool and went along with it.

When he said, 'Chooks, what pizza do you want?' I'd notice myself in conflict. While the real me wanted to say, 'I don't want pizza, I'll make myself something else,' my voice would say, 'Peri peri chicken, please.'

At that stage I was in good contact with my observer self. She noticed that while I *knew* what I really wanted, I had difficulty vocalising it and, as a result, went with the easier option. I observed how I was doing this one thing and asked myself, *If I'm 'being cool' with eating pizza when I don't actually want it, then what else in my life am I 'being cool' about when really, I don't want it?* Now, many years later, I not only don't eat pizza, but I'm also vegan (on rare occasions, vegetarian). Making space to listen to and support the choices the 'real me' needs has meant many changes in my life.

My hesitancy in saying, 'I'm good, I'll make something else,' was due to the story in my head telling me not to be 'difficult, hard work'. I told myself that if I behaved that way, and Steve caught wind of me being a 'drainer', then he'd leave me. That was the story playing out in my head. *If I'm difficult, aka not agreeable, not easy-breezy-beautiful-cover-girl-type shit, then he'll leave me. So in order for him to stay, I must be agreeable.* Fucking ew. But also, hello Little Kat in me somewhere, probably in her tender teens, who needed to be heard, have me sit next to her and have a chat.

When you realise how toxic not honouring your true self is, it's tempting to beat yourself up. But it's also important to be tender with ourselves. To understand that wounds from the past created this story for a reason: to protect. Throwing methylated spirits on old wounds is *not* the answer. But tending to them, carefully and kindly, will eventually help them to heal.

One of the best ways to do this is to be present. It may be the greatest gift we can give to ourselves. Our presence is our essence – the ground floor of our being. By being present, we enable the observer in us to watch ourselves as if we were watching a movie in which we are the main character. In the observer mode we allow ourselves space to be curious about our behaviours. It allows us to feel our discomfort in speaking up, saying no and owning the ways we go about life. It then invites us to go deeper, to explore and mine our own mind, stories, ego and wounds; to tend to what is there. By separating ourselves from our stories, ultimately, we can liberate ourselves.

In this case, liberating myself meant saying out loud that I wanted something else. It meant saying I didn't want to eat pizza and realising this great gift: that I can stay true to me *and* be in a loving relationship and be loved. I didn't need to bend like a pretzel and be inauthentic. There were no ultimatums and I didn't need to choose one or the other. Observing the way I did this one thing tapped on the front door of my wounds, ego stories and limiting beliefs around relationships. The pizza was my invitation into the work.

Get this tool into your life: Self-enquiry

What tennis match is going on inside your head? What has woken you up at 3-fricken-am and kept you worrying so much that you can't go back to sleep? At the level of deep visceral truth, what is this *really* about?

Perhaps you're doing your head in about people taking advantage of your goodness to the point of deep-seated rage and resentment. You rant to yourself, *Why do I do this? Why won't I learn? Why do people take advantage of me?* You want this behaviour to change and you're seeking greater clarity about it.

This is when we create a 'self-enquiry question'. In this case, it could be something like, *If I was someone who knew my worth, held my boundaries and honoured my time, how would I and life be different? What practices would I have in place to be this person?*

Then you take this question inward, get quiet and breathe.

You settle into a state where you surrender yourself to new information coming in.

Play a beautiful song.

You give yourself a moment for your body to be part of this.

There's no need to send out a search party for the answer.

There's no need for your mind to find the answer.

Rest back into your body, your senses, your knowingness.

Let the answer find you.

Meet Megan

Let's see how Megan, one of my legendary clients, worked with the Self-enquiry tool.

Megan was in all sorts about her work, wondering whether, due to toxicity in the workplace, she should leave or stay. Pregnant with her first baby, she'd been treated as if she were dispensable. The company had changed its path, its actions weren't living up to the values they publicly projected, and she was backed into a corner of either choosing to come back to work full-time with a newborn or find another role. She'd worked at this company for five years and loved it. She thought the world of her work and feared she'd never find something as good again. Fear kept her there, but her entire body was saying, *This is no longer for you.*

I'm sure that reading this, it seems obvious she should leave, but her ego story was running rampant and kept her in psychological stress for almost nine months. Nine very painful months. We all know how paralysing indecision can be. She could see it and I could see it, but the tennis match of indecision in her head kept her in doubt. The pros and cons list wasn't providing any clarity and when she sat in front of me, I saw sheer exhaustion and frustration on her face.

Megan often relied on her head for answers and guidance, which is cool. But . . . when we're seeking deeper answers and deeper guidance beyond logic and reason, we have to take the short walk from our head to our heart.

'Grab your pen and journal,' I said, 'and let's do a practice of getting quiet, enquiring and making space for truth to come forth. We gotta get you out of your head and into your heart.' Just saying that aloud made her body relax.

At the top of her page, I asked Megan to write the question: *If I knew what was true and good for me, what would that be?*

Framing it in this way unplugged the question from, *Should I do this or that? Is this decision right or wrong?* In doing so, we moved away from seeking certainty to appease anxiety to instead land in her place of knowing. Asking the right question makes a world of difference. It's a practice called self-enquiry.

Self-enquiry stops the tennis match inside your head when you're trying to make a choice. This is not to say the mind is bad and that logic isn't good, because it all has its place. But when it comes to what really matters to you – the way you want to live and the pace and rhythm you want to move at – then deep self-enquiry is a precious and sacred practice. As spiritual teacher Mooji reminds us: *Self-enquiry is not asking you to believe or to trust – it is putting a mirror in front of you and asking you to look.* Look and you shall find, because what you are seeking is also seeking you.

I played soft, gentle music, asked Megan to close her eyes, get quiet, breathe and invite in her senses by paying attention to what she could hear, smell and feel. In this state of presence and emptiness, I reminded her of the question at the top of the page. When she felt ready, she put pen to paper and wrote.

The tennis match in her head had stopped and the answer was staring her in the face. There was no, *Is this right or wrong?* because she just *knew.* Her whole body relaxed, her eyes softened and there was visible peace in her being. Who she had become and the place where she was working no longer aligned – that was the bottom-line truth. While her authentic nature had expanded, her place of employment hadn't. Though aligned in herself, she had been rocking up to somewhere that felt wrong for her. What she really wanted, deep in her heart, was to create a way of life where she could work and raise her children with time and space. At her rhythm, her pace. That was her authentic way.

Megan and I caught up two weeks later and she had resigned, giving herself space to breathe again. Ever since, she had been flooded with new, fresh and exciting creative ideas. Awesome at branding and design, she had created a logo and started some sketches. Although she didn't know what lay ahead, she had a sparkle in her eyes and an excited curiosity about what would happen next. She was creating her life!

Chapter 8

Self-compassion and self-worth

Embrace your done-ness

It's a moment many of us know all too well – that crossroads where we're done with how it is (the state of your life, relationships, work, money, health, headspace or outlook), fed up with the way things have been and ready to pave a new way. Reaching our moment of complete and utter 'done-ness' isn't about succumbing to despair or giving into self-criticism. No, it's a sacred invitation – a call to awaken to our truth and let it rise all the way through us, to the very surface.

So what does it mean to reach this breaking point? It's a moment of reckoning, a soul-stirring realisation that the way we've been showing up, being and acting in the world no longer aligns with who we truly are. It's a profound shift in perspective – a recognition that there is more to us than meets the eye, that we are worthy of so much more than we've allowed.

Even amid our deepest despair, we must do our darnedest to approach ourselves with kindness and compassion. It's easy to beat ourselves up for reaching ground zero, to berate ourselves for not seeing it coming sooner or facing it sooner. But that's not the path to true liberation. Instead, we must embrace our total done-ness as a catalyst for change – a wake-up call to step into our authenticity with courage and grace.

It's not your fault

One morning, I was sitting at home by myself, watching *Oprah* (the good old days of having only three channels to choose from). I would have been around eighteen. Mum and Dad were on an overseas trip and my brother had moved out of the family home. It was just me and our two dogs, Sootie and Minnie. Oprah's guest, a psychologist, was talking about sexual abuse. Oprah shared her own experiences with sexual abuse and the psychologist said that people who have been sexually abused need to know one thing: *It is not their fault.*

These five words silenced everything around me. This one sentence delivered the words I hadn't known I needed to hear. They were the hug I needed, the open arms I craved to comfort and hold me. The words were so simple they broke me open. They broke everything that I was trying to hold together, everything I had been running away from.

Tears of relief poured out of me. I finally got the god-given memo: *It was not my fault.*

When my parents came home, an overpowering need rose in me to be real and honest. I knew that, once and for all, I had to face my past and my demons. I had to acknowledge and look at what I had shoved so deep inside for so long. This time, I needed and wanted my parents' help. I was willing to invite them into my pit full of pain. Little did I know I was going to be invited into theirs too.

It was time to speak my truth. To be heard. To be supported. To release this pain from me. I told my parents that I wanted to talk about something important and took them to dinner at a local restaurant. I didn't want the conversation to happen at home – I wanted a neutral place where voices couldn't be raised and doors couldn't be slammed. Somewhere that was familiar, but not home-environment familiar.

Although I had told my dad the story years earlier, I had never fully admitted the pain it caused me and how much shame I secretly carried. For the first time I admitted just how deeply the abuse had affected me. I told them it was *still* affecting me, how I was suffocating on the inside and that, until I heard that sentence on *Oprah*, I had somehow believed it was all my fault. I told them that I needed to heal and that I needed help in doing that, because the pain I was carrying was taking over my life, my sanity, my *everything*. I asked for their help. I meant it. They could see in my eyes that I needed their help like never before. They had tears in their eyes. They were listening. They were there. They were holding my hand. They were deeply sorry.

My parents vowed to help me however they could and asked for my permission to tell my brother. When Dad spoke to Matt, I felt as if I had been violated all over again. He told Dad that it had also happened to him. That same holiday, that same babysitter had abused my brother too. He was nine years old at the time. You can imagine how hard that hit my parents, how hard it hit all of us. With our secrets exposed, though, I finally had validation that I wasn't crazy and that I had indeed lived this traumatic experience. My brother's moment of being real and honest made our whole family get real and honest and, as a result, our individual healings began.

Healing would take so much longer and be so much more difficult than I realised going into it, but even if I'd known this, I would have done it again. I could no longer tolerate the pain of not facing it. But man, going to see a counsellor and talking about my past stirred up so much shit.

We did an exercise called The Empty Chair. The counsellor encouraged me to imagine anyone sitting in that chair and to say out loud what I needed them to hear. She suggested a few people to get me started, giving me full permission to not hold back. Finally, she suggested putting my abuser in the chair. To this day, that may be one of the hardest things I've ever done.

Later that night, I called my brother. I really, really missed him. I said, 'I don't think I can do this, it's too hard. I feel like I'm unravelling and have so many feelings to deal with. I want to go back to how I was before.' He listened, held space and let me have the moment.

I'm done!

I now know that this part of the process is normal, natural and makes sense, even while being so hard and ultra-frustrating. Of course, we want to run back to what is comfortable, what we know, what we think is safe – even if that reality sucks. We want to undo the realness, undo the honesty and undo the doing that takes place when we summon change. We want to repel the tidal wave of repressed feelings and emotions that are now coming in thick, fast and randomly and, at times, inconveniently. This is where we can freak out, seek to gain control, turn our backs on deepening our authenticity and sabotage. But like I said: it's normal, it's okay. It's an expected part of the journey. It's a test to see what you'll do.

Do you run and try to forget the truth that has finally found its way back to you? Or do you withstand the discomfort, seek support and guidance, and learn new ways of handling the ick, the mud, the blackening darkness, the dark nights of the soul?

The women I work with all have those moments of *Fuck, what have I done?* An ego freak-out moment where reality is shifting and changing around them to match the 'them' that awaits. Even though what awaits is far better, far calmer, far more exciting and more liberating, the desire to run back is real. This is when I remind them that they are in between two states. Not fully in the old, not fully in the new. They're somewhere in the middle being stretched, pulled forward, pulled back, amid a messy, turbulent storm, simultaneously holding on and letting go.

How do we come to that moment of *I've had enough! I'm done, I'm so done living this way! I can't go on like this?*

Done with editing yourself to the point where you can't even recognise yourself or look into your own eyes.

Done with screwing yourself over and contorting yourself to make others' lives easier who have zero interest in anyone other than themselves.

Done with offering up your precious time and energy to those who benefit from your 'saying-yes-without-even-thinking-about how-this-will-affect-you' syndrome.

Done with moving through life so damn fast that you don't even taste your food, your coffee, the morning air. Rushing to everywhere and everything acting all busy and that you've 'got no time'.

Done with being scared of what might show up for you, inside of you, worrying if people will still like you if you are grounded, quieter, more still and say 'no' to serve your wellbeing.

Done with holding yourself and others up to unrelenting standards.

Done with saying that you want a real relationship yet when a good egg comes along, you push them away and nit-pick and find everything wrong with them because your ego can't bear the thought of real love.

Done with avoiding, defending, blaming, victim-ing and pointing the 'you're the problem' finger at everyone else, life, the universe.

Done with being someone you think you have to be, to be more likeable, palatable, acceptable, good and all the rest, where it's costing you your freedom and stunting your self-expression, your soul's evolution.

What does it take for us to feel 'shook to our core', as if something in us is shaking us by the shoulders to 'wake up' and realise we're a shell of who we are? What does it take for us to realise that we've been living a life that doesn't feel right, good or true for us, to the point we cannot ignore it anymore?

I talk to my clients about the 'cumulative effect', where something is gathering or growing gradually. This effect can work in two ways; either in favour of us, or not. We could be doing things over time that serve us. Eventually, something great and wonderful takes place in our lives (which is what we'll focus on in this chapter). Conversely, we can be doing things over time that don't serve us and, eventually, it reaches its peak and something happens that rattles our world (thank you, ego). From the time we were young children we have been adapting, tweaking, pruning and contorting ourselves to survive and respond to our environment. We've been resolving difficult feelings we don't know how to hold through sophisticated strategies and adopting a persona that 'helps us get by'. Ex-haust-ing.

Me, myself and I

Ever since the age of fourteen, I'd had a boyfriend. Being by myself with my own thoughts was a terrible feeling and attaching to someone felt safe. But after six years, at age twenty-five, my longest relationship ended. I was lost. Completely unused to being alone, I felt very uncomfortable, so I attached to a friend. I needed guidance, company and someone around for comfort. The cumulative effect of losing myself in others was nearing its peak, I just didn't know it yet.

At age twenty-seven, I began dating a guy from Sydney who was so not right for me, so not good for me, so not true for me, but my ego was a fan. He was pulling back on the text messages, not calling as much, and kept saying how busy he was with work. One night at a party my friend said this Sydney guy needed to go and that I needed to be more empowered to make this choice.

That night, a guy at the party took an interest in me. In my truth, I wasn't keen on him. I actually wanted to be at home with my family and think about what my friend had said but my ego wanted to be wanted. I took myself off to bed and while I was asleep, the guy came into the room and started making out with me. Nothing in me wanted this, but I went along with it. I felt cheap, dirty, used. Bathed in shame.

When I woke the next morning, I just wanted to get out of there. My friend was disappointed in my behaviour, not understanding why I let that happen and realising how easily influenced I was. At the time, even *I* didn't know why I went along with it but it's clear to me now!

My friend distanced herself from me for some time which left me no choice but to be with myself. I knew there was no other way.

No other person to attach to. Those days were done. I knew it in my bones. It was me, my thoughts, my feelings, my mess, my heart, my soul. My 'cumulative effect' moment had arrived and it was time to do the inner work. There was nowhere else I could go but *in*.

In that space, I could see how potent my ego stories were in allowing others to take what they wanted or needed from me, and how not speaking up, standing my ground or even having something to stand for, left me disempowered. In that space, I looked across the span of my life and the patterns that had played out, the pain my behaviour caused myself and others, and how I was showing up. It was time to learn a new way, so I could come home to the real me.

To this day I (my ego) attempts to sabotage where I'm headed. It throws me stories, narratives and fear around where I'm going and pulls out the evidence files as to why 'this isn't a good idea'. I tell you, it's relentless.

Let's use the example of when I wanted to get real and honest about how I was showing up in intimate relationships. Why? Because after nine months of dating guys and it ending after six weeks, time and time again, I thought the male population were a bunch of arseholes. Then, I had one of those awakening moments. Not quite a brutal awakening but it was a hard pill to swallow. I realised that the common denominator was (ughhhhh) me. It became clear that I was showing up on dates pretending I had all my shit together.

I portrayed a happy-go-lucky, independent, all good, no drama-llama chick who was not prepared to show up as I was. I'd morph into their likes and dislikes which left no room for them to get to know me. Then, behind closed doors and after dates, I'd be doing my fucking 'nana in, waiting for them to text. I'd be in the shower with the ringer on loud in case they'd message. I'd imagine text message sounds and would check my phone. (Don't laugh, I know you've done that too!) And when my mates messaged instead of the guy, I was so disappointed. Yeah, not so happy-go-lucky after all!

So, if I was going to get real and honest about shifting this, my next best step was to date myself, like myself, be okay in my own skin and company, and rediscover what I liked and enjoyed. I'd go on solo brekky dates, drive to new suburbs and walk around the shops, go on day trips to the beach, and people watch. And all the while, my ego would say, *No one will like you for you, you have to make it easy for them, you have to be the non-drainer kinda girl, blah fkn blah!*

Get this tool into your life: I'm Done

For real, the next time you are in a hole of despair and total overwhelm, I want you to get out a pen and paper and write down what you are done with. It'll look something like this.

Here's what I'm done with . . .

1. Hating my body and withholding loving it until it looks like 'this'.
2. Not letting myself take a moment to sit on the couch and enjoy a movie because I always need to be 'doing something'.
3. Calling myself fat, ugly or never accepting a compliment from someone.
4. Being passive and waiting for the universe to knock on my door and deliver everything I want.
5. Not asking for what I want in case I don't get it.
6. Not enjoying sex and making it a chore as opposed to something that might in fact liberate me.

Go on and on as long as you need. Write with as much anger, frustration and done-ness as there is inside of you. Get the done-ness out of you and onto paper. Then, let it rest. Let the stir that took place inside and on the page rest.

Once you've had a moment (and by moment, I mean a few days) of rest from your done-ness, take your pen and write at the top of a fresh page, 'I am deeply sorry for . . .' The sorry is towards yourself, the authentic you that your ego has trapped in the basement. It'll look something like this.

I am deeply sorry for . . .
1. Speaking harshly and unkindly to you.
2. Not letting you listen to your body when it needs to rest.
3. Not allowing you to see yourself as beautiful, exactly as you are.
4. Not believing in you and what you're absolutely capable of.
5. Withholding your dreams.
6. Withholding pleasure.

A deep apology for every done-ness. Once you're done, let it rest too. Clearing and acknowledgement can offer profound healing and homecoming. When it feels right, maybe in a day or so, take your pen and finish this practice off with writing, *I love you, please forgive me, thank you.*

Meet Claire

Claire wanted to do just about anything to get rid of her ego. In her first session she said, 'Kat, I want all the negativity gone, completely gone!'

I said, 'That ain't gonna happen.'

Most of our time together was spent helping her to come to terms with and accept that no matter what she did, who she saw or who she was in the presence of, even if it were the Dalai Lama or Oprah, her ego, stories and limiting beliefs weren't going anywhere. Claire learnt instead to work with them and then to choose something greater. She learnt to expect that as she went for the great, her ego stories would flare up like an old dormant rash that she'd need to tend.

At first, she didn't like that. You see, she wanted to never have to tend to that damn rash again – the stories, the darkness, the shadowy shadows. She only wanted the great, which is fair enough. I mean, me too, Claire! But alas, that is not the way in this existence. Yes, there are those who 'love and light' everything and spiritually bypass the dark, but that doesn't really solve the problem. In truth, that practice is ignorance wrapped in spirituality. I know, because I too was spiritually ignorant.

Claire needed to face her ego, learn from it, understand its purpose, realise how every situation in her childhood informed it, grew it and loaded it with more and more reasons to do as it says to stay safe. We used a number of tools to help Claire accept this part of her. One of these is the Write Your Ego a Letter tool.

Bonus tool: Write Your Ego a Letter

Sometimes, it can help to go deeper, like writing-to-your-ego deeper. Below is the first letter Claire wrote. She was a bit unsure of where to start, what to say, if what she was writing was the 'right thing' or if she was doing it correctly. I reminded her that this wasn't about a perfect letter with perfect sentence structure or perfect paragraphs and punctuation. It was a letter to express outwardly what was going on internally. 'Let go, Claire. Then write from that space.'

Dear Ego,

I have hated you for so long and wished you away. You've brought so much pain and suffering to my life, or the life I am not living because you won't allow me to live it, or even go after it, but I am here to end our war. I don't want to fear you, fight you or spend all my years trying to get rid of you. I am here to make peace with you, or at the very least try my best.

My intention is to understand and accept why you are the way you are, heal the little Claires who were and are in pain and who informed you, so I can have more compassion and empathy for who I have been. My intention is to expand beyond the way you see me, my life, and life in general. My intention is to find the real Claire that I know is in there, somewhere. My intention is to be at peace with you and be comfortable in the real me, all at once.

I'm sure the road will be rocky and difficult, but I am here for it. I know you might struggle with this and I'm sure I will too, but I will find new ways to manage you, listen to you and acknowledge you as I make a new path. May we do this with greater ease, greater understanding, greater patience and grace. I am ready for a new way.

Sincerely,

Claire

Chapter 9

When the light goes out

The in-between wobbles

You know that feeling – the one you're left with *after* the home truths have come at you full steam without reprieve. After you've dealt left, right and centre with old ways of thinking and doing. After you've wrestled past-you demons that had zero desire to change. After you've dragged your ego along with you as a new you emerges into the light.

It's a feeling of relief and hope that resurfaces after ploughing through what seemed an eternity of heavy sludge. A feeling of, *Oh, okay, I'm okay! The world isn't falling apart, my world isn't falling apart (anymore), my life isn't over, I'm not crazy, I can breathe again!* A sense that you're occupying more of yourself, more than you ever have, feeling into new parts of you that you're still getting acquainted with, but which all feel good.

You're not quite fully stable and grounded yet, but it's coming, it's happening. That feeling is the *transition* feeling. The in-between-old-and-new feeling. It's new, empowering and raw. It's that wobbly period after you've cocooned hard and battled old ways, when new ways are emerging. When you know it's time to let your new wings (insights, downloads, perspective, intuition on steroids, et cetera) out into the world. It's a time to respect, to go easy and find your footing as you become reacquainted with the next layer of your authentic self. A time where you are metaphorically naked and heightened in sensitivity. It's normal and it's okay to go slow and steady.

Your voice might sound different, at times you'll wonder what you said and where it came from and you'll feel so attuned to your surrounds that it can be overwhelming and beautiful all at once. This is normal, this is okay, go slow and steady. This wobbly period of time is your rebirth into the world as your renewed self after what feels like going through the ringer of life, aka the dark night of the soul.

When will you learn, Kat?

Just when I thought I was getting my shit together and heading towards the path of sorting out my life, there was one final kicker for me to battle. This one got me in the teeth and brought me to my knees.

Remember that nerve pain that shot through my body when I was out partying? Well, from the ages of eighteen to twenty-three, that became full-blown chronic nerve pain, head to toe. I relied heavily on pain medication to get me through it and continued my job as a nurse until it started to become unbearable. For anyone reading this who knows what it feels like, or knows someone who has chronic nerve pain, it's the fucking worst. It robs you of your life, slowly taking away the spontaneity and freedom you once had to go out and dance, or work a night shift, or party late with your mates, take a walk or do anything that might light you up. It slowly takes away your spark, your joy, your hopes, your dreams, your spirit.

When I went into hospital nursing, I had stopped the party drugs. I did, however, switch over to prescription medication. What started out as taking Panadol for the pain quickly turned into Panadeine Forte, Tramadol, Endone and Valium. I'd never take the medications on a shift but when I got home, my body was ruined. I couldn't get comfortable and no matter how I positioned myself, the pain was still there. I'd have pillows under my back, my legs, my arms and hope to hell that the medications would knock me out. The medications didn't really take the pain away but they made me all fuzzy in the head which helped me not think about what was happening in my body.

Over my nursing years I worked in Cardiothoracics, Children's Cancer, Neonatal ICU and I did some nursing via agency placements to experience variety. When I was twenty-two, I was at the Royal Children's Hospital and some mornings I'd walk up the stairs to my shift. There'd be times my eyes would flicker, I'd miss a step and think, *Mmm, that's kinda weird!* Little Miss Avoidant led the way and dismissed it, putting it down to shift work, tiredness and not sleeping well due to the pain. There were times when my thumbs would swell and one side of my body would feel like lead. I knew something wasn't good but didn't want to make a big deal of it. Hello old patterns of shoving shit so far down that you fool yourself for a little while that 'all is well', and smile and nod and hope to hell that you don't get a glimmer of that truth in your consciousness.

Shift work was exacerbating the pain. After coming home one night, I took a Valium and my whole body wouldn't move. I was talking myself down to try and calm myself but I was so scared. After it wore off and I could move again, I spoke to my parents about leaving shift work nursing to find something that was more nine-to-five where this pain wouldn't be an issue. I was acknowledging that this was bad but not enough to actually investigate the cause. You know what it's like, sourcing outside of yourself to fix the shit inside.

I got a job as the head nurse at a plastic surgeon's office – a great guy I always called 'Doc'. It was a lovely and calm environment, decked-out rooms with music playing and candles burning; it was so different to hospital nursing. Aware of my pain, he sent me to different practitioners. But nothing took the pain away.

One busy day, Doc and I were heading downstairs, as we usually did, to get the next patient. I was at the top of the second flight, Doc was at the top of the first flight. I stood there, unable to move, unable to make my foot take a step, unable to connect my thought of, *Move your foot*, to my foot to make it move. He looked up at me and said, 'What are you doing? We need to get the next patient!' I looked at him with fear-filled eyes and said, 'Doc, I can't walk!' The way he looked back chilled me to my bones. This was bad.

Before I knew it, I was having an MRI. Movement returned and I could walk again, but there was no *Oh, she'll be right* attitude this time. Reality was getting very real and honest with me, and I had no choice but to be real and honest back. *Fuck, another gnarly wake-up call! Why didn't I tend to this sooner? When will you learn, Kat?*

The pits of despair

If you haven't heard about it before, let me introduce you to the 'dark night of the soul'. It's a place we fear to enter, a realm of shadows and uncertainty. But make no mistake – it is also the birthplace of profound growth and awakening.

Welcome to rock bottom, the gauntlet of transformation. That moment when everything we thought we knew, everything we held dear, comes crashing down around us, leaving nothing behind other than raw, naked truth. It's the feeling of utter despair, of being lost in the wilderness of our own minds. It's the culmination of years, maybe even lifetimes, of suppressed emotions, unresolved traumas, and disregarded whispers of the soul.

Welcome to a harrowing period where everything you'd previously thought made sense, doesn't. Where what you thought was your path comes into question. Where what you believed to be important, vital and of value is now under the microscope. It's a period where everything you once thought stabilised your life and made you 'you', collapses, and no matter how hard you try, you can't clutch on to 'save' or 'keep' it. To put it simply, it's fucking rough.

But here's the thing: the dark night of the soul serves a purpose; a vital, essential role in our journey to self-realisation. It's the moment in which our old selves are melted down like the Wicked Witch of the West when Dorothy pours water over her. We're stripped bare and reborn. It is the ultimate test of our resilience, our courage and our capacity for a new way.

It's easy to coast through life when everything is going according to plan (whose plan?), when everything in life seems to be squeaky clean, like *The Truman Show*. But it's in the darkness, in the depths of our despair, that our true character is revealed. It's in those moments of rock bottom that we are forced to confront the parts of ourselves we've long ignored – the fears, the wounds, the shadows lurking in the small spaces of our psyche. And yet, it's also in those moments that we find our greatest strength, our deepest wisdom, our most profound compassion.

If you find yourself standing on the edge of the dark night of the soul, know that you are not alone. Know that this too shall pass, even when it seems like it won't. Know that on the other side lies a new dawn – a new beginning. The darkest nights give birth to the brightest stars.

What have you lost in the dark?

In the depths of the dark night of the soul, it's not uncommon to feel as though we've lost our minds. We find ourselves drifting in a sea of uncertainty, grappling with questions we can't quite answer yet. But perhaps even more unsettling is the realisation that what we thought was important to us may no longer hold the same significance.

You see, the dark night of the soul has a way of stripping away the illusions we've built around ourselves: the masks we wear, the roles we play, the possessions we cling to. It's a reckoning with the essence of our being – a confrontation with the truth of who we are, beyond the trappings of ego and expectation. We realise through this period that things we *thought* were essential maybe aren't. That friend from high school who tears us down more than they celebrate us. That person you've been dating who says all the right things, but whose actions prove otherwise. The job that sucks so much time, energy and life force at the expense of your personal life and wellbeing. Acknowledging this is scary. The person you thought and believed you were, whom you relied on to get you through life is now in question. So now what?

Although the darkness feels like a devastating loss, it also brings opportunity – opportunity to rediscover what truly matters, to realign ourselves with our deepest values and desires, to reclaim our sense of purpose and meaning. There are the things that have been lost for many years, ready to be claimed by you. It's a process of excavation, of digging deep into the recesses of our soul to unearth the buried treasure.

So how can we begin to see what we've truly lost and work towards recovering it? First, you let go of what you *thought* was essential. As you watch it melt away, what remains is truth. Then, you go into honest introspection – a willingness to confront the uncomfortable truths beneath the surface. It means asking ourselves the important questions: *What do I truly value? What brings me joy and what doesn't? What am I willing to let go of in order to live in alignment with my authentic self? Who am I willing to become?*

From there, it's about taking action – taking the next best step towards reclaiming what's been lost, slowly slowly, whether it's rekindling old passions, nurturing neglected relationships, or forging new paths. Even in the darkest of nights, there is light to be found.

During one of darkest periods it became essential to my soul to seek dance. I had danced since I could remember, but somehow I'd lost its joy. I was at dancing school from the age of four – jazz, tap, ballet, you name it. And I bloody loved it. But I clearly remember an audition where I heard my teacher say to another, 'She'll never be a prima ballerina.' I felt my heart sink and wanted to stop dancing right then and there. It was one of the first memories I recall where I doubted myself and believed someone else over my own truth. From then on, I still enjoyed dance, but it became more about getting the moves right and comparing myself to others rather than enjoying the music, how my body moved and how I felt.

By the time I was eighteen, dance was about clubbing, taking party drugs and hooking up with people. By then, I'd lost the essence of dance and myself in the process. I didn't find it again until I was twenty-five, when I first experienced 5Rhythms, a dynamic movement meditation practice devised by Gabrielle Roth and based around five states of being: Flow, Staccato, Chaos, Lyrical and Stillness. I was deep in self-discovery mode, desperate to end my people-pleasing antics and was open to just about anything to bring me back home to my authentic nature. But the idea of a bunch of sober humans in a hall, free dancing and seemingly not giving a fuck made me want to run for the hills. My judgement of them was real; of the music, the place, the space. Nice protective antic, ego. By this time, though, I was aware of my ego's sneaky ways and I stuck with it. After twenty minutes of doing my absolute head in, I too eventually gave zero fucks and was hooked.

Until that moment, I'd forgotten the power of music, rhythm, movement and the freedom that comes with letting your body move how it needs and wants to. I've done a lot of healing, mindset work, meditation and therapeutic treatments and I tell you, dancing with your spirit is top of my list for creating unbelievable shifts and a deep relationship with our true nature. 5Rhythms was the invitation back to myself. It gave me permission to not give a fuck-in-sight about what my head was saying. That practice of giving zero fucks to the stories in my head snowballed beyond me and out to my community – so much so that I created my own dance events.

At my ZEROFKS dance events, it is one of the greatest sights to see people who walk in timid and shy, move into doing the side-step or a little pop of the shoulder and standing at the edges, to going all out, singing at the top of their lungs, right in the middle of the dancefloor without an ego fuck to give. Seeing humans in their natural, relaxed state is profound and never fails to take my breath away.

For the last twelve years I've kept dance close to my heart, letting it teach me more and more, to rock 'n' roll in my own life to my own pace, my own rhythm and find the beat of my life. Not others' lives, or society's timeframes – but mine. I continue to hand myself over to its healing ways. Little Kat is a big fan of this. For me, dance is life!

Little Kat beams inside when I go to Afrobeats (an incredible blend of West African music with American jazz, funk and soul), dance at home in my space, dance in the streets when I'm singing to myself, dance in the queue when I'm waiting for something. I'm not talking about a full-out routine, I mean just a little shoulder groove, just a little head bop, a little torso movement to connect my body to a killer beat. At home, I'll play a range of songs that immediately pang my heart with joy, excitement, freedom or whatever it may be. I give myself over to the music, the beat, the rhythm. My ultimate song is 'This Is Me' sung by Keala Settle from *The Greatest Showman*. That song is my anthem. My coming-home song. My 'Yes, this is me!'

What is your soul crying out for you to reclaim? What will make it come alive again? Do you dance, even if you think you can't? Do you play a legendary song that activates every cell in your body where your bones say, *Dance!* When no one is home, do you bang out a tune and let it all go? Do you go to a local dance class to try out your moves? As an in-home nurse, I once cared for a woman with motor neurone disease. She could only move her fingers and head, and she could speak. I cleaned her home, made her tea, did her shopping. But what she wanted more than anything was to move. She said, 'Kat, can you put some music on and dance with me?' And when those tunes played, she moved whatever she could. '*This* is what brings me the most amount of joy, Kat!'

What is it for you? You know the thing I'm talking about. The thing that makes your soul say, *Yes! This is it, this is what makes me feel alive!* Is it swimming in the ocean? Is it sitting on the comfiest spot in your home with a piping hot cuppa by your side as you knit, knit, knit away? Is it putting on your hiking boots, packing a backpack and some water, and heading out for a day in nature? Is it painting, creating, losing yourself in some kind of craft? Cooking, being around animals, singing with others, singing solo, looking after your plants – what is it for *you*?

Get this tool in your life: Three Good Minutes

When I was at my lowest, even doing something for three minutes felt almost impossible. Almost. But even at my worst, I could do something good for three minutes. Three minutes of anything that could get me out of my most negative thoughts, that could break my stuckness. To this day, whenever I'm feeling out of sorts and disconnected from my true self, I take a moment. I consciously redirect my attention to doing something that I know can help me regroup. All it takes is three good minutes.

Three good minutes of standing with your feet on the grass, eyes closed, hands on your heart.
Three good minutes of listening to a song that takes you straight 'home', standing, swaying, feeling.
Three good minutes of sitting on a park bench, watching the world go by, listening to the birds, the trees, life.

Three good minutes of finding the sun's light in your home, standing in it and letting it warm your face.

Three good minutes of putting your feet in a body of water – the ocean, a creek, a puddle.

Not every one of these needs to be done every day; it's more a matter of choosing three good minutes in your day to do something that brings you home. That gives you that feeling of, *Ahh, there I am.* Three good minutes where you find yourself, say 'hi' to yourself and feel good that you're still there. Because three good minutes a day is better than no minutes a day. It's better than nothing, isn't it? It may seem small and insignificant, but in practice, it's the small and insignificant things done consistently that makes the big, significant shifts.

Meet Jacqui

Jacqui, a fifty-something-year-old legend of a human, was trapped inside her very (very) good girl persona. Not a foot out of place. Not a word spoken without over-consideration. Not a single question of *What would I like my life to be like?* A woman married to a man who'd been unfaithful for almost ten years, who wore it, buried it, made it okay in her mind, not telling her nearest about it, pretending that all was 'fine'.

All was fine to her ego. *This is how you do life, no questions asked!* Until something in her wanted to ask, wanted to question, wanted to enquire, wanted to dig deeper, wanted to let out what seemed to be long gone. She centred our work on this challenge:

I realised that I was holding myself back. I was scared to go and try something that I have wanted to do for a long time, so that is what I set my challenge about. I am researching some dance schools and have made enquiries this week, so hopefully will be putting myself out there in the coming weeks.

You mentioned in your tutorial that doing these things will be challenging, hard and we will have setbacks. This has all resonated with me, but I am persisting.

Strangely, today, I have just sat and listened to the meditations again and WOW, did I get a rude awakening. I thought I didn't really give a fuck about what anyone thought, but I have not been truthful with people for approximately ten years about the situation that I have been living with. I have glossed over everything and not been at all authentic. This has to change, I cannot pretend anymore.

Jacqui and I worked together for almost two years. When I first met her, her unhealed younger selves ran her. When we finished up, she was a woman who tended to her younger selves when she observed, noticed and became aware of inauthentic Jacqui. She looked at herself candidly for the first time in years, finally left the family home and found herself a new place. She travelled solo and went on long road trips and hikes, something she had never done. She danced, oh she danced, over and over and over again. She danced in nature, on her walks with her dog, finding her beat, her rhythm, her spirit. And with each look in the mirror, each step she took toward her independence, each road she travelled, trail she hiked and dance she danced, she found her way home.

Chapter 10

Finding our way home

The homecoming

When we think of 'coming home' we usually think of travelling back to comfort and familiarity from places faraway. In a spiritual sense, the travellers are your lost selves. You ejected them when your ego-persona was in charge. You denied their existence. But through the dark nights of the soul, you learnt that denying the shadows only prolongs the pain. You realised that rejecting parts of yourself isn't the answer. The homecoming is your summoning call, inviting your lost selves to return, welcoming them with your whole heart and allowing them to find space within you.

Now that you're awake, you will spend the rest of your life journey reclaiming and retrieving 'lost yous' along the way. Certain situations, interactions or people will activate something inside of you and you'll feel a nudge, a telling vibe that quietly says, *There's something here for you to look at*. There are many 'yous'. Many whom you've said so long and farewell to, due to some story you have around them. Maybe the 'you' who was laughed at in school, or was told was too loud, annoying, or intolerable. Maybe a 'you' who was ignored, taken advantage of, or made fun of, so you packed them up and sent them on their not-so-merry way.

These 'yous' are the parts of you that, when you think about them, make you cringe, scrunch your hands up, feel ick in your stomach, or filled with anger, shame or embarrassment.

But as you take this path, you'll see that there should be no part of you that is left behind or remains buried. This journey comes with ownership of *all* of you – the wounds, the scars, the cringe and the outstanding – bit by bit, layer by layer. When one lost self is reclaimed, in time the other lost selves will seek to be loved, accepted and reintegrated back into your life.

Stuck in the zombie zone

We waited twenty-four hours for the MRI report to be sent over. None of us were brain doctors, so Doc sent it off to Mr T, neurosurgeon. Shit was getting even more real. Mr T read the report, called Doc and said, 'I'll see her tomorrow at 6 pm in my rooms.' Usually, getting in to see Mr T would take three, sometimes six months. This flipped my stomach. I thought, *Hmm, maybe this is going to be a bit more than getting a few weekly massages and some acupuncture!*

Mum came with me. She met me at work and we walked over to the hospital across the road. We stood in the elevator and she held my hand and prayed. I thought we'd go in, Mr T would tell me I'd need some kind of therapeutic treatment and we'd be all fine and dandy. The cumulative effect was about to dispel my delusional fairy tale. We were told that I had a congenital brain malformation known as Arnold-Chiari, with large syrinxes (fluid-filled cysts) in my spinal cord compressing the nerves and causing damage and chronic pain. 'You'll need surgery as soon as you can to correct this to stop the progression of side effects, possible permanent nerve damage and paralysis,' said Mr T.

I was twenty-three. By this stage I'd been living with chronic nerve pain that had been growing in intensity for the previous five years which, like I mentioned before, had slowly and progressively taken over my life. I was moving less, for fear I'd be in pain. Going out less, for fear I'd be in pain. I took many pain medication pills, for fear of being in pain. I went to bed early so I could fall asleep at a reasonable hour, for fear that the pain would be so bad that I wouldn't get comfortable for hours. I was gaining weight, losing what was left of my spark and becoming jaded about life. I thought so many times, *What the fuck have I done to deserve this? Am I a bad girl? Which karma god has it in for me? What did I do wrong in a past life? Is this the way it's going to be, forever? Because if it is, I'm fucking out of here!* Not only was my physical health in trouble, but my mental health was the worst it had ever been.

Surgery was my only option, so surgery it was. I said to Doc, 'I'll resign. I'm new and am already a burden, find someone else!' He said, 'Katrine (his nickname for me), we'll see you when you're ready to come back.' I worked my arse off to have everything sorted and ready for the nurses who covered for me. I loved my job, my boss, my work colleagues and I wanted to make it as easy as possible for them while I took six weeks off.

They came to see me in hospital regularly. My family were by my side, especially my mum. We were all so hopeful that this would work and be successful, and to an extent it was. Structurally, my neurosurgeon did an A+ job and what was previously jammed up was now free flowing. But as the weeks went on and the weaning off the medication gave me the opportunity to feel how my body *really* was, the chronic nerve pain remained. Fuck me. To put the cherry on the cake, I was readmitted to hospital post-surgery with extreme headaches to the point of being unable to see. Due to leaking of the cerebrospinal fluid, I was blacking out.

I went to so many different practitioners I can't even count them on two hands. My neurosurgeon said that this pain would be something I may have to manage for the rest of my life. *Ahh, are you for real, dude? How the hell do you expect me to live like this for my remaining years on planet Earth?* At this point I thought it was a total shit hole (sorry, Mother Earth). *How, at twenty-four years of age, do you expect me to manage this? With pills? By staying indoors and not moving because I don't want to be in more pain? By saying no to going out with my friends because I'm too conscious of being a drainer? By having sleepless nights because I can't get comfortable in any position? If by 'management' you mean that, then I want out of this existence.* That's where my head went. If this were to be my life then I was utterly done.

My neurosurgeon suggested a medication that had helped patients he'd treated, but there were some side effects to be aware of. Dizziness, drowsiness, depression, blurred vision, fatigue, weight gain, dry mouth, headache and impaired balance. I was concerned by these, even though I'd taken way worse drugs in my heyday, but the pain was crippling, so I took the medication. The pills took away my pain, but they also took away my soul. I was vacant. Zombie-style vacant. Staring-at-walls vacant. Everything was dark. I felt no joy, no connection, no light. How was *this* life? Nothing in me felt alive. I was dulled, dimmed and numb. I felt dead.

I thought I had lost myself before. This time, the zombie zone was far worse and far deeper. I lost myself in a bottomless pit, and honestly, I couldn't see how I would ever escape.

The truth is, there *is* no escape

Where I was going wrong, what I hadn't yet learnt, was that I couldn't run away from my broken self. All the pieces of me that I hated, that I wanted to bundle up into a garbage bag and throw in the bin were the pieces of me that I needed to integrate into my life. I hated them and didn't want them, but I needed them more than anything else.

Given my childhood trauma, it's understandable that I developed a love/hate relationship with my body. During my late teens and early twenties I allowed people to treat my body however they wanted and gave it up freely. In my later twenties and early thirties I swung the opposite way, became closed off and dressed to say, 'Not interested, off ya pop!' I also cut off all my hair to say, 'I'm off the market, mate.'

This was my ego's way of protecting me from being seen as an object, weak and a target. It was Little Kat, unhealed, needing to protect herself from the world with an invisible *Don't fucking touch me!* sign. But it inhibited my self-expression and denied my sexual needs and pleasure as if to say, *Nah, don't need that – I'm good, thanks.* Fake authenticity. All the way to the end of the spectrum of Little Miss Independent. Still, ego. I didn't want anyone to take my power away again, so instead, I took it from myself. At that time in my life, I saw being feminine as weak. It made sense to hide what it meant to be feminine.

In 2022, I was asked to speak at an International Women's Day event in front of 250 women. Kindly, the company sent me an outfit to wear. It was simple and beautiful, just the way I like it, except the skirt and camisole top also happened to hug my body. Like the ning-nong I was, I wore a shirt over the top to 'cover up' my décolletage and shoulders. I walked in feeling like the outfit was very revealing and screamed 'look at me', when in actual reality, I looked beautiful.

The other women in the room were also dressed beautifully and I admired them, complimented them and was inspired by what they wore. *How come I applaud them, but condemn me? How come I think they can wear that gorgeous dress, show skin and look sexy, but think I look like a slut?*

During the night, as I observed my thoughts, I began to allow myself some distance from them. Eventually, when I realised how badly I was treating myself while applauding the other women, I finally gave myself permission to take off the shirt and feel free in my body. Then, the drummer in the band came up and started dancing close to me. He was just being friendly, but I turned and walked away, got my shirt and put it back on. Ooft, was I in for some serious self-reflection over the coming days!

The lost self that was asking to be reclaimed was my femininity and allowing myself to express that through what I wear. As I used the self-enquiry meditation and journalled on this, it became clear that I have used clothes as my boundary to communicate, *I'm not a sexy or sexual person, so stay away, thanks!* This voice was Little Kat, the girl who reluctantly wore dresses to church, who was sexually abused by a disturbed churchgoing babysitter. Little Kat said, 'Cover up, buttercup!'

This guest-speaking engagement was another 'shake my shoulders' wake-up call to a lost part of myself that was waiting to be reclaimed. It brought me back into harmony, presence and life. Being authentic is to own *all* of you. Not just the 'good bits'. Not just the 'please-able' bits. Not just the 'likeable' bits. Not just the 'easy' bits. With that reclaiming comes healing, a deep and meaningful *I'm sorry, please forgive me, I love you, thank you* message to yourself. This act comes from a traditional Hawaiian prayer called Ho'oponopono, a reconciliation and forgiveness that is very, very precious.

Making peace with your ego

I often hear people talk poorly to their ego, telling it to 'shut the fuck up', 'drop dead', or 'take a long walk off a short pier'. I get that it's an infuriating part of us that is forever putting up stop signs followed by a barrage of reasons why it's not safe to open your heart, or that you're not ready yet to audition for a role, or that your art isn't perfect enough so keep working harder. There are days where I want to perform an ego-ectomy and live happily ever after. But alas, this isn't a Disney movie and I'm no surgeon.

In my earlier years, I too would yell, kick and scream at it, do ego-burning fire ceremonies to wish it away for good, only to be deeply disappointed that there it was again the next day. In a nutshell, I was fighting it and fighting it until I learnt that this gets you nowhere other than frustration land.

It may seem counterintuitive to befriend your seemingly inner enemy, but please remember, the ego is simply fulfilling its job description. If the ego were an employee, it'd get promoted at its performance review because, sheesh, it sure goes above and beyond its duties. When it flares, and it will, remember that your younger self made many decisions to 'not do that again' and 'next time we'll do this'. It did this because at that time you were hurt, either physically, mentally, emotionally, spiritually or all of the above. The meaning you gave that situation informed and grew the ego, created a protective shield around your heart and buried your authentic nature, deeming it to be the problem. *Put that aside, you won't be needing that! You've got to be the tough one, the achieving one, the dominant one, the subservient one, the peacekeeping one.* Separation from the real you is its MO. So when the ego's memory is reactivated and it takes its usual precautions to try to protect you, take a moment to remember that it is simply replicating what it did to protect you earlier, thinking that it still works. It doesn't realise that at this time in your life, that approach is no longer the solution.

When it comes to reacquainting yourself with your authentic nature, a huge part of the journey is developing patience, compassion and acceptance of the ego. Think about it. For years it has rejected your authentic nature, hiding it from you, others and the world. And look how that turned out. Just because you are aligning more closely to your authentic nature doesn't mean you reject the ego. We don't play tit for tat or seek an eye for an eye. Instead, we welcome all parts of ourself back to the fold. We embrace the two opposing forces within us that have been seeking dual occupancy, each waiting to be held, acknowledged and honoured in their own right. Our ultimate goal is to no longer reject our darkness, wounds and shadows, or our radiance, essential nature and inner truth, but rather, harmonise these polar opposites.

Get this tool into your life: Ho'oponopono

Ho'oponopono is a traditional Hawaiian prayer and healing practice deeply rooted in the concept of reconciliation and forgiveness. In its original context, it was used by Indigenous Hawaiians to resolve conflicts, restore harmony within families

and communities, and promote inner peace. The prayer empha-
sises the importance of taking responsibility for one's actions,
acknowledging mistakes and seeking forgiveness from others.

Today, Ho'oponopono has gained widespread popularity as
a powerful tool for personal transformation and healing. It is
often used as a mantra or meditation practice to release negative
emotions, clear energetic blockages and cultivate a sense of inner
peace and wellbeing.

The prayer itself consists of four simple phrases: *I'm sorry.*
Please forgive me. Thank you. I love you. These words are repeated
internally or spoken aloud, serving as a powerful reminder of the
transformative power of forgiveness and love in our lives.

Here's where you might use this practice in your own life:

During conflict resolution. When tensions arise or conflicts
emerge in relationships, use the Ho'oponopono prayer to dis-
solve resentment, restore harmony and foster forgiveness. Let
the prayer soften you.

For self-healing. When grappling with self-doubt, guilt, or
emotional pain, turn to the Ho'oponopono prayer to nurture
self-forgiveness, self-compassion and inner peace. Let the
prayer soften you.

In relationships. Whether it's with partners, family or friends,
practise the Ho'oponopono prayer to mend strained relation-
ships, heal past wounds and nurture deeper connections. Let
the prayer soften you.

When letting go of the past. When haunted by regrets or past
traumas, embrace the Ho'oponopono prayer to release nega-
tivity, make peace with the past and move forward with clarity
and grace. Let the prayer soften you.

Amid stressful situations. In moments of stress or anxiety, use the Ho'oponopono prayer to cleanse negative energy, restore balance and invite calmness and serenity into your life. Let the prayer soften you.

For intention. Use the Ho'oponopono prayer as a tool for aligning your thoughts, intentions and actions with positivity, abundance and divine grace. Let the prayer soften you.

As a daily practice. Incorporate the Ho'oponopono prayer into your daily spiritual routine or mindfulness practice to cultivate a sense of inner peace, gratitude and spiritual connection. Let the prayer soften you.

Meet Tessa

Tessa came to me fed up. Fed up with thinking something was wrong with her, that she had every mental disorder under the sun and that she needed serious help to get better. She had leant on the 'I'm broken, I'm unfixable' story for so long that she was diagnosed with multiple mental health disorders and medicated. She's a fellow Enneagram #4 The Individualist, like moi.

For years she lived in her story thinking, *This is who I am, this is how I am, this is how I will be.* She'd research her symptoms, see a professional, convince the professional she was 'not right and needed something to fix her' and voilà, she'd get something to fix her. Except, it didn't. Tessa held high hopes and felt temporary relief that the medication would make her normal. It eased the sting of anxiety, the wide swings in mood but the story remained.

'Kat, at my core I know I am not as fucked as I tell myself, and that I'm not as crazy as I keep convincing others that I am when

I'm stuck in my ego. How do I make peace with the story in my head that doesn't get the memo?'

Bit by bit we popped her ego illusions using a myriad of tools from awareness practices, reflection questions, naming her Enneagram type and patterns. Slowly and surely, she dropped into herself. She was able to distinguish story from reality and identify how much she lived in story as opposed to reality. She very slowly came off the medication with the guidance and support of her naturopath and psychiatrist, realised that she wasn't bipolar, depressed or had multiple personality disorders and found stability and grounding in her authentic self. She had never experienced so much peace, so much stillness and so little drama. Now, she's in the practice of being herself in her relationship and not causing fights based on story. Her practice is to be *with* her partner, to feel what they already have and not pick everything apart and deliberately find fault. No more imagining, *Something is wrong in our relationship.*

Tessa used the Ho'oponopono prayer to apologise to herself for believing something was wrong with her, to forgive herself for taking joy, presence and peace from her life, to love herself wholly and truly as she is, and to thank herself for coming back home. As Emma (Chapter 6) and many of my clients do, Tessa also used the One Good Question tool. 'What lives beyond the story of I am broken, I am fucked up?' she asked herself. 'What is *that* Tessa like and what does she have to say?'

PART THREE

LIVING
AUTHENTICALLY

Chapter 11

Answering the call

Lay down your swords

Fight, fight and fight you might, but at some point you're going to get tired of fighting. Fighting yourself, fighting the life that's looking for you, fighting the new way that awaits, fighting the real you.

Surrender is the moment when we lay down our weapons, release our grip on control, and open ourselves to the wisdom of the universe. It's a journey that many of us embark upon reluctantly, for we've been conditioned to believe that success is synonymous with struggle and that victory is earnt through sheer force of will. But here's the truth: sometimes, the greatest battles we face are not fought with swords and shields, but with the very fabric of our being.

We fight and fight and fight, until we can't anymore. And in that moment of *no more*, of surrender, something miraculous happens – space is made for what we truly seek, where we can begin to honour our true selves, to answer the true callings of our heart. It's a revelation that shakes us to our core, for it is in surrendering that the new way reveals itself – a path illuminated by the light of our authenticity, our purpose and our passion.

Why is surrender so essential to our journey of self-realisation? It takes courage to let go of the familiar, to relinquish control, to trust in the unknown. It's a recognition that we are not separate from the universe, but intrinsically connected to it – that when we surrender, we align ourselves with the flow of life, with the rhythm of the cosmos (as woo-woo as it sounds, somewhere in you, you know this to be true). And in doing so, we unlock the door to what awaits us at the level of the heart.

Surrender is not a one-time, one-and-done thing, but a lifelong practice. It's a daily choice to surrender to the wisdom of our hearts. And with each act of surrender, we inch closer to our true selves, to our true calling, to the life we were always meant to live.

If you find yourself weary from the battle, if you find your spirit longing for peace, know that surrender is not defeat, but liberation. It's the key that unlocks the door to your deepest desires, your wildest dreams and your highest potential. Embrace surrender, embrace the unknown and trust that in letting go, you will find everything you've been searching for.

Asking for help

Six weeks after surgery, I returned to work. After taking the medication my neurosurgeon prescribed, I was horrible to the patients and horrible to the people I worked with. I was horrible to my family and my friends. I was horrible to *me*. Everything was black. Jet fucking black. There was this defeated, dominating voice inside me that said, *What's the point? There is no point. If this is it, then I'm out.* I wanted to check out of this place called life.

My work colleagues were so concerned that they suggested I take time off and talk to my family. I was pushing people away.

I didn't want anyone close to me. I did want people to feel sorry for me, but I didn't want them to feel sorry for me at the same time. My thoughts were chaotic and complicated. Little Miss Independent, Little Miss Avoidant and Little Miss Needy were at war.

When all the Little Misses dropped their guard for a moment, I wrote my parents and brother an email:

To the people who matter most,

I feel it is important for me to let you know how I am doing at the moment.

I know I don't have a life-threatening illness like cancer and people think because I am young that I should be coping better and that I look well, but at the moment I am not. I am not coping, and I am not well.

I have been in chronic, severe pain for almost six years and I have reached a point where it is affecting me mentally. I can see it and feel it in my personality and it upsets me.

I am not patient, I snap more (than I did before), and I have a care factor of zero for most things in life which is what has slapped me in the face to change!

To wake up with the pain I have set my mentality to, 'How am I going to get through today?' I already feel defeated, like there is no hope or point, and I do not want to be that type of person.

I want you all to know this because I don't want you to think that I am just an angry, short-tempered person. I want you to realise that living with chronic pain is physically and mentally a struggle. But I want to rise above it!

I am looking for someone who can help me cope with my mental space because that is my greatest concern.

Love,

Neng x

My dad replied:

From one of the persons who matters to another,

    I can only imagine how you might feel after such a long period of enduring pain in the varying forms it has been with you . . . and I care a lot about what impact it may have on you. If I could wish it away it would already be gone and I applaud the step of getting some professional help with how your mind can cope while you continue to search for a permanent solution. You have been very strong and your decision to seek help is another example of your determination to get on top of this. It is not easy to be honest like you have in identifying the impact this is having on your life.

    Please let us know what we can do to help you along the way. You are very precious to all of us and our concern just doesn't stop with the question, 'How's your back?' We're in this together, Neng, and whatever way we can support you, know we will. We will never allow this to defeat your beautiful spirit and reading your email rips into my heart. We will never, never, never give up on a complete recovery for you so let's get started on creating a list of all the things that can be done and get working on them one by one.

    I love you and pray that all the positive energy is with you at this time.

    Dad xx

This was my surrender. It was a deep plea for help; me reaching out in desperation. I had been pushing people away and this was my way of telling my parents I needed them (can you see my pattern?). I needed the support. I needed their help. I needed to do something. I knew that somewhere in the beyond beckoned a life worth living, but I also knew I couldn't get there on my own.

I knew there was more than this, that there was more to life and that this way of living was not *it* for me. There was more to life than pain, suffering, shoving truth inside, keeping people away, abusing myself and people-pleasing. There was more than abandoning myself. Something in me knew that there was more, that there was something beyond this place of pain and suffering.

I'd had enough of my own misery and pain, and I finally listened to it. I didn't numb it with drugs or push it away with egoic patterns. I had to get to the rockiest of the rock bottoms to listen to the still inner voice, and I finally listened. I was a resistant turd, I know.

Perfectly imperfect

Deep down, and for some, maybe it's way, way down, I believe we yearn for a world that is kind, considerate, caring and loving. We strive to live in such a way, to approach life in a manner that is wholesome and authentic, to offer our best intentions for others, our planet and ourselves. Do we always practise this? Hard no. Does that mean we're terrible people? No. Do we slip up and revert to unkind, inconsiderate and unloving ways? Yes. Why? Because we have our good old pal, ego, who holds deeply entrenched and fixed views about the way life works, how people are people and how you have to behave to get some needs met.

The stories it'll come up with will go something like ... *Why bother offering to help others, they're ungrateful bastards! Screw being a good person, people take advantage of that. What's the point in signing petitions, picking up rubbish, composting: the government controls us anyway! The world is fucked and is going to end soon! Why bother being kind to people? Do you know how many people have hurt you, why should you be nice to them? There's more evil than good out there. Humanity will never change.*

And you know what, maybe it won't. But is that a thought you're willing to rest on? Are you really willing to go through life giving no fucks about doing what matters in your heart? Does doing nothing feel right, good and true to your authentic self? The reason I direct you towards your heart is because, to our egos, a *lot* of stuff matters. Being right. Being the most powerful. Being of importance. Being 'the nice one'. Being 'seen and not heard'. Being the loudest. Being the most perfect. Having the most achievements and plaques and letters after our name.

However, our egos and our hearts prioritise very different matters. Just look up the Enneagram work again and see what our egos are focused on when we're down in the unhealthy levels of development. To the ego, only *our* needs matter and the mayhem we can cause in order to get those needs met is kinda frightening. I mean, all you need to do is take a sneak peek out in the world and see it happening.

If you've had thoughts like this about life and humanity, it's okay. I have thoughts like this all the time. Even as I write this book my ego voice is saying, *This book isn't going to do jack shit for people. Humanity is unsalvageable, don't even bother!* But, unfortunately for my ego, I've been on a quest since 2009 to live true to myself, and even though these thoughts get me down, I remember what matters and what I stand for. I surrender my ego and gently encourage my authentic self to rise again.

Get this tool into your life: Surrender

There are times where you will be so over it, so done fucking with yourself. You'll be tired of your own wicked sorcery and desperately willing to give up the stories that keep you contained, that hold you in the pleasing, the overachieving, the dominating, the perfectionating, the peace maker-ing, the silencing, the belittling, all-the-ing patterns. When I reach this point, I have not a drop, not an ounce, not a pinch more energy to carry the story. I am all out of fucks to give. I don't want to fight the new layer of authenticity that is ready to reveal itself. I don't want to resist what's calling me. I don't want to stay in the loop that's driving me fucken crazy. I want out.

It's in these moments of surrender where I willingly hand over what my little human self has been trying to hold onto and control, and I write . . . One way you can do this is through writing a letter from the desire in your heart to align closely with your authentic nature. In your own time, grab a pen and write your own letter or, use the one written below as a starting point. It's a letter my kinesiologist first shared with me, that acknowledges and honours both forces with discernment, kindness and respect.

Dear Life,

Please take from me that which does not nourish my soul and that which is no longer right, good and true for me. I allow the forces of love to take this and decide for me. Give me the courage to say thank you and goodbye to what has been and no longer will be.

Love,

Me

That's it. Leave it there. You have nothing left in you but trust and faith because you're done. This is often the hardest practice and there might be an almighty fight before surrendering. You'll know when you've had enough of your own self. When that time comes, hand your shit over. Let it go.

Meet KG

KG, a client, now friend, was an A+ student and jumping out of her skin to abandon herself and be a Little Miss I Will Bake for You, Cook for You, Adjust My Timetable for You. She was a say-it's-okay-when-you-cancel-the-date kinda gal. She is a dead-set legend of a human, but when it came to guys, she acted from deep in Enneagram #2 The Helper.

When we first worked together, KG wrote down all her dreams and aspirations and I said to her, 'No love?' She looked at me as if to say, *Fuck off, Kat John, don't look at what's not there, look at what's there!* But that's not how I roll. KG had left love off her list because she couldn't bear the thought of it not happening. If she left it off, then she didn't have to feel the pain of love not working out for her. To resolve this we went deep into her patterning, examining the steps she took each time she met a guy where she felt she simply could not be herself because being herself was not enough to deserve love. Heartbreaking stuff. Through reflection, journalling, self-enquiry, meditating and piecing it together, she saw her patterning and the moment when the switch flicked from 'I'm cool being me' to 'you are not enough, so you must act as though you are more'. Being real and authentic became high on her values list because she simply couldn't desert herself one more time.

KG had one final test before she met the love of her life (not joking, she is now with the love of her life), a guy who seemed a little different from the others she'd dated before, who was kinda up for dating, and kinda not. He'd say, 'Let's go on a date' but not follow up, so KG would follow up on the day of the date, he'd push it out to a later date and again, not follow up. She saw how she was about to bend and do the limbo on herself to 'make it okay', but it wasn't. It wasn't okay. Her authentic self had come to the forefront and said, 'Enough is enough, voice how you feel and let him go'. To her giant credit, she did. She put authenticity into action, into real-earth time and made it matter. She made *her* matter. One step forward for KG's self-respect, one giant leap for her sense of worth.

Chapter 12

Living to account

True to the core

Living authentically isn't only about managing your head, ego stories, automated patterns and reactive behaviours, although that's a major part of it. It's also about getting back in touch with your core self. And one of the best ways to do this is to get back in touch with your core values.

Our core values are the deeply ingrained principles that guide our actions. They matter immensely because they're the very foundation of a life that expresses our most authentic selves. Think of them as the roots of a strong tree. When we nurture them and align our actions with these values, we are standing firmly and rooted in our truth. It's a way of saying, without needing to say, 'This is who I am, this is what I'm about and this is what I stand for.' Over time, your values may flex and grow. As we mature and move into different stages of life, our priorities may shift a little, just as branches sway in the wind. But their true essence will remain.

So what happens when we lose touch with our core values or, worse, when we compromise them? It's like shaking the roots of that sturdy tree: chaos comes a-knockin'. We find ourselves feeling out of sync, stressed and disconnected from our true selves. In this state, we make decisions that don't reflect who we are, leading to a life that doesn't align with our authentic nature, which leads to feeling even more crap about ourselves.

On a broader scale, when our society and world operate out of alignment with their core values, we can 'forget' our humanity. We turn on each other, hurt one another, look only at our differences, tear down forests, wipe out species, point fingers, seek dominance or revenge, hide truths, sell lies, and quite literally give zero fucks about the soul that resides in another being, in the land of our mother and in all species. We do and say deeply hurtful things that fracture and erode trust and faith in humanity. We hang our heads and shake them in disbelief, and think, *To hell with this place!*

At times like that, it's tough, but I urge you to not hang out with those thoughts for too long. In these moments it's essential to regain sight of your core values. They will help keep you focused and give you strength, even in the midst of the storm. They will be your guide and your anchor. Without them, you will sail rudderless, lost at sea.

Values are the bedrock

In our always-on world full of distractions, pressures and competing priorities, it's all too easy to lose sight of what truly matters – our core beliefs, our guiding principles, our moral compass. Our core values are the bedrock upon which we build our lives, the foundation upon which we stand. And in a time when our fragile society seems to be fraying at the seams, it's more important than ever to take responsibility for our choices, to be accountable for our actions and to live in accordance with our deepest, truest values.

So what does it mean to find your values and live true to them? It's a process of peeling back the layers of conditioning and societal expectations to uncover the truth of who *we* are and what *we* stand for. It's about taking a long, hard look in the mirror and asking ourselves tough questions: *What do I truly believe in? What principles do I hold sacred? What legacy do I want to leave behind?*

But finding our values is just the first step – the real challenge lies in living in alignment with them. It's not always easy. It requires courage, integrity and a willingness to stand firm in the face of adversity. It means making difficult choices, even when they're unpopular or uncomfortable. It means taking ownership of our actions, acknowledging when we fall short, and committing to do better next time. It means holding ourselves to account, not just to others, but to ourselves.

And yet, living true to our values is also incredibly empowering – it's a declaration of our authenticity, a testament to our integrity, a beacon of light in a world that often seems dark and jaded. It's a reminder that we have the power to shape our own destinies, to create the kind of world we want to live in, one choice at a time.

Know that you have the power within you to reclaim your sovereignty, to pave a path that is true to your values, and to live a life of purpose, passion and meaning. Embrace the responsibility that comes with that power, embrace the accountability that comes with that responsibility, and know that in doing so, you will contribute to creating a world that reflects the very best of who we are.

The invisible prescription

The email to my parents was a desperate plea for help. Because of my willingness to be real and honest about myself and my life, and finally, to share it with them, I knew this time, something would change. My family rallied around me and they fought for my freedom too.

At the time, Mum was volunteering at one of the busiest and most respected teaching hospitals in Victoria. Through colleagues, she found someone who was close with neurologist Professor J. It usually took around six months to see him, but I saw him in four weeks because I was such a royal mess. Finally, something was working out for us. This is when everything changed.

My referral email to the professor went as follows:

A colleague at work has a daughter in her twenties who has intractable headaches following surgery for an Arnold-Chiari malformation about a year ago.

She has been pumped with narcotics by doctors and has been told there is nothing left to do.

She is desperately trying to find a way out of being narcotic dependent, etc.

I know this is not your gig . . . but . . . I think she needs to be seen by a neurologist to rule out any residual organic causes and she needs to be seen by a caring individual who may refer her on to the right person if they are not able to help her themselves.

I figured you might know someone else who can help you help her once you have excluded things that need to be excluded.

She called to make an appointment and the earliest she could get in was March. I took the liberty of asking your receptionist to bring her forward to January.

Sorry for referring you such a challenging case . . . but I figure you are the only person with the mixture of knowledge/common sense/open mind that might be able to help her.

Here. We. Fucking. Go! In no time I rocked up to the professor's rooms with Mum and Dad. In my mind, I thought I'd be having more surgery, or be put on more pills. That's what I had pre-loaded. I really didn't think he could offer me anything.

But after going through my history and circumstances, Professor J told us he thought it was possible for me to live a pain-free life without surgery. Then he told me that I had to want it. I was like, *Ah, dude, I want this, of course I want to be out of pain. Why the hell do you think I'm here?* He kept chatting to me and made me realise that although I'd been telling myself I wanted the pain to end, I hadn't been doing anything proactive to change it (cue reality slap from professor). I had been so focused on not wanting to be in pain – avoiding it, taking medication, retreating from life and socialising, not moving my body – that I was actually totally focused on it.

Professor J taught me a life lesson with a beautiful analogy. He said, 'When Olympic athletes train for a gold medal, they do whatever they have to do. Every day, they'll eat, they'll sleep, they'll train, they'll rest. They do whatever is necessary to get that gold medal because they want it so intensely. They visualise it, they work towards it and they achieve it.'

I got what he was talking about but I was also looking at him thinking, *I'm not an elite athlete!* But he knew that just as they wanted to win gold, I too wanted something. He asked me, 'As much as an Olympic athlete wants to win gold, what do *you* want, Kat?'

I sat there, Mum and Dad either side of me, and said, 'I want to be free. I want to be free to be me – to smile, to dance, to enjoy life, to walk, to laugh, to do what I want!'

'That right there, Kat,' said the professor, 'is your gold medal!'

Professor J had offered me an invisible prescription. He asked me to train every day for the next twelve months for my gold medal. He instructed me to visualise what I and life looked like when I was free and happy, when I could do whatever I wanted and be who I was born to be. I was to visualise this and feel what it felt like and then act in accordance with that vision. It was a cycle of visualise-feel-act, visualise-feel-act, visualise-feel-act. Professor J advised that, in his experience, after twelve months of this daily training, I could be pain-free, but that I needed to 'train' with the same tenacity as an Olympic athlete. Over the twelve months, I had the option of continuing to take the pain medication I was on, but I wanted to stop it and fully commit to this new prescription. I wanted to go all in! 'All in' kinda suits my personality.

So I committed to the full twelve months, but I had to fight the demons of negative thoughts and self-doubt, and what I now know as my ego – the part of me that was trying to keep me safe. Wanting to keep me tied to my identity it kept telling me this was not going to work, that I was going to have a hard time if I didn't take my medication, that I was going to be bad at this ... that I would fail again! That I'd be a bitch to the people at work if I didn't take my pills, that I'd be in shocking pain if I went down this path. As many self-inhibiting thoughts as you can think of, that's what went on in my head.

Living your values

Living in resonance with your values will create true harmony in your life. When your behaviours and inner truth align, that is authenticity. But in this world of conflicting ideas, how do we know what is true for us? I ask myself the following questions, because that's what matters to me, and this is what knowing your values can do for you.

- When you shop, buy clothes and products, think about whether they resonate with your values. What are you supporting? What are you encouraging?
- What chains of behaviours are you keeping alive that cause unnecessary harm to humans, animals or the planet? Is it good for humanity? Is it good for the planet?
- Is it good for animals? What life did they live? What death did they endure?
- What environment were these clothes made in? Do the people who make these clothes get paid, see their family, get a lunch break? Are they greeted by name, acknowledged with eye contact?
- What resources were used to make the $2 cup, or top, or bath bomb? Did Earth's Mother cry and weep for her precious resources?
- And did we even like the cup, the top, or the bath bomb? Did we use it or keep it, at least for a while?

Two of my core values are kindness and impact. When I shop, I think about what impact I'm having on the planet and if there's a way I could be more considerate and kind. I shop predominantly at a store called Gram Sustainable in Elwood, using the empty bottles or containers or egg cartons I have at home and refill what I can to reduce waste. We compost at home and I tell you, my bonus daughters are dead-set legends when it comes to this. They take reusable bags to the shops, containers to the butcher, and compost like bosses. At the start, they were like, 'Huh?' Now, they're on it. I'm actually in the process of connecting with a farmer to buy meat directly from his family for my family. We're setting up a meet and greet on the farm to see how they do things, treat and feed their animals, and what happens when it's time for their lives to end. Even though I don't eat meat, I don't want to contribute to factory farming and with greenwashing at an all-time high, what is written on packages, in my view, can't be trusted. Free-range doesn't always mean free-range.

Steve calls me Councillor Kat, because when I see things in our community that have little regard for the animals and the planet, I am straight onto the council. I actually use an app called 'Snap Send Solve' which is very cool. You take a picture of bins overflowing, for example, note the location and send it directly to your council. And I gotta say, it works! I care deeply about being a respectful custodian of the lands on which we live. Rather than say, 'It's not my problem' or, 'Someone else will sort it out!', I use my frustration to drive action. Sure, it can be hard to adjust to new ways of doing things to align with your values, but I believe it's much, much harder to live out of alignment.

Over a period of eight years, I went from eating meat to living vegan. The value of kindness spoke to me and nudged me to be accountable to what I stand for. I love animals and couldn't stand the thought of how they are treated, kept and handled in factory farming, used for entertainment, drugged to be patted and photographed with us – the list goes on. This is the shit that keeps me up at night, that has me clenching my fists and tears filling my eyes. I can't bear to think of an animal in pain at the hand of a human. I went from eating all meats to only white meat, dairy and fish; then to only fish and dairy; to just dairy; and finally, to veganism. It was gradual, slow and steady. I copped shit from my family, questions from friends and became the 'energy drainer' at the dinner table for a while. But I was prepared to face that because living my value of kindness was more important. In the same breath, the value of kindness also means being kind to myself. When I've eaten out and the vegan options have been pretty average, I've eaten vegetarian to ensure I fuel my body with good food. It's always a dance.

Now, it has opened up a new community for me and opportunities to represent brands that also take this stance. When we stand for what is deeply true for us, our outer world begins to match our inner world. The forces move and shift, realigning people, life, circumstances and opportunities. People will enter your life who align with you, while others may distance themselves because they don't understand or resonate with you or your values.

When you first start trying to live your values, there will be a transition period from the way you've been to what you now want to embody. You'll be challenged to live with integrity, authenticity and congruence. This may look like standing up for matters you were once silent about, taking a new approach towards your children, your partner or even yourself, saying 'no' to a plan you already said 'yes' to because your wellbeing is not so well, or choosing to go about your life in a way that is slower, more present and more considered.

During this transition period, you'll experience egoic resistance and, possibly, external questioning. People who know you might say things like, 'What's with the not drinking anymore? What's with the going to bed early shit? What's with the sit down and talk about our feelings business? What's with the eating all clean and healthy? What's with the you speaking up all of a sudden? What's with the eating less meat? What's with the quitting your job and taking a year off?'

I have copped every single one of the 'What's with the . . .?' queries. In the beginning of the shift, I felt the need to explain, defend, not totally stand up for it and own it, or blame it on some lame reason. I was awkward and uncomfortable in finding my new feet. No doubt, you'll get them too. As these comments fly around, you may also feel 'something' pulling you back to your past behaviours (and we all know by now what that something is). You know what you want, yet the outside and inside voices start up. It can feel like an internal tug of war; there's pulling and pushing at the same time. This is normal, all good and part of it. It's the transition phase.

Knowing your values

If I asked you right now what your core values were, could you state them with ease? Or might it take you a minute to search through your 'I know I did them but I can't remember them for the life of me' files before saying a few out loud? Maybe you know what they are as you recently did a values exercise . . . but are you in touch with them, for real? Are you in a relationship with them? Do you check in with them? If you are for real on this authenticity path, then you gotta be in contact with your core values. That means living them, breathing them and noticing when you feel in conflict with them.

Our values get us back in touch with our truth. We are in a world that is predominantly built on how to be successful, earn a stack of cash quickly selling just about anything, and on gaining peak popularity. Sadly, it doesn't focus on important values that benefit us, other people and society. Do you want to be part of that problem, or help show the way, the real way? It's all intercon-nected, but we forget, then fail to put our values into practice. The more people who listen to their truth, tune into their values and see the chain reactions of their choices, the more we *all* grow.

Let's say that in your heart you value authenticity. Maybe in the past when you've gone on dates, you have donned different personas (like moi) and adapted yourself to thinking and assuming that they like 'this', so let's hide 'that' about yourself. By doing this, you've put forward the false you, which your ego doesn't mind, because its agenda is: *I'd rather be rejected for being fake than being rejected for being who I really am.* Now, though, after discovering how important being authentic is to you, you want to show up on dates as yourself: open, honest, confident, relaxed in your being and owning what you want for your life.

After knowing this to be right, good and true for you, your ego might leave you alone for a bit . . . until it's time to go on the next date. For as long as you've allowed it to rule you and your behaviours, it has never related to you as your authentic self. It sees your identity as a chameleon, a people pleaser, a human trans-former that'll morph into whomever it needs to be to gain a 'like' from someone you might not even respect! So here you are, caught between the two selves. One who stands for being liked at any cost and the other who stands for being authentic.

Get this tool into your life: Your Core Values

Are you a living, breathing, walking, talking example of your core values? Do you lead by example? Are you embarrassed to take a stand for something and, if so, why? What ego story is there? If you want to be one of those people you are mesmerised by because they are so solid, grounded and so 'them', then you already know the answer. Knowing, defining and living into your core values is imperative.

Don't be that someone who preaches one thing and does another, because people's bullshit radars are stronger than you think and when something is millimetres off from the truth, something is bound to feel 'off'. You will feel it too.

It can be hard, sometimes, to unearth your true values. Based on a guided meditation I often deliver, the exercise below offers a way to unearth yours. Start by centering yourself with some deep breaths, then let's begin.

Using the beauty of your imagination, I'd love you to imagine that deep down inside of you there is a special box. Maybe sometime in your life you had a glory box – a box where you kept things that really mattered to you, things you wanted to savour and look back over. This is such a box.

This box inside you has the energy of treasure, of something special, important and which matters. You can feel it all the way down, at your deepest centre.

You know it's there and maybe it's a box you've hidden from yourself.

You know it's there, but you've been busy.

You know it's there, but you've just got so much stuff to do.

But now that we're here, now that you're present, we're going to take time to reunite with the treasure that rests inside that box.

So imagine journeying to your deepest centre where that box resides. Make your way there easily, pleasantly and with curiosity, with eagerness.

As you're moving closer you feel its energy, you feel its frequency.

It feels familiar. You know what's inside of it.

As you move closer to the box that stores your deepest truths, you know what resides there: your five core values.

Core values that relate to the you that you are now.

And those core values make up what matters, what truly and deeply matters to you.

As you open the box, what's revealed to you are the things that matter, that you treasure, that you dare to stand for, that you back, that you believe in, that you yearn to prioritise.

As the observer, watch what comes out of this box.

Accept it, take it in.

Then, whenever it feels good and true for you, take out your journal pen and begin to write down what is coming out of this box – what matters to you, what's important to you, what you value.

Take your time here. You may start with a long list of ideas, but ultimately you want to distill them down to a maximum of five so it's not too overwhelming. If you have more, they'll tend to overlap.

When you have settled on your top five core values, reflect on them and begin to define what they mean to you. Look up in the dictionary what each of your chosen words means, then make your own meaning of them.

Ask yourself if you are living into these core values currently.

Write down a 'next best step' to get you further into the practice of each core value. As an example, here are my five core values. I'd love to encourage you to write out yours, using the same format.

1) Kindness
How do you define this value?
To be aware of and consider my impact on all life forms (humans – myself included – animals, the planet).

How will you live into this value?
Ask myself, is what I'm about to say or do kind towards and considerate of another being's life?

Why does this value matter to you?

Kindness is the cornerstone of our humanity, extending its reach to all beings, human and non-human alike. Acts of kindness serve as powerful beacons of light, illuminating the path to compassion, empathy and understanding. Whether a comforting word, a helping hand, or a simple act of generosity, kindness has the remarkable ability to uplift spirits, mend wounds and forge connections that transcend barriers of species, language and culture.

2) Authenticity

How do you define this value?

To be true to myself and be as unedited as possible.

How will you live into this value?

Be aware of the people I feel less comfortable around, determine why that is and make one small change next time I am around them that honours being authentic.

Why does this value matter to you?

Authenticity is the essence of our being, the unedited expression of our true selves in a world often defined by conformity and pretence. It is the foundation of genuine connection, allowing us to relate to others from a place of honesty, vulnerability and integrity. By embracing our authenticity, we not only find liberation and fulfillment within ourselves but also inspire others to do the same, creating a ripple effect of authenticity that touches all beings and enriches the collective human experience.

3) Impact

How do you define this value?

To create a lasting feeling in people's hearts that inspires them to live with integrity.

How will you live into this value?

To show up grounded in who I am, what I stand for and own that, trusting that my essence will impact another's.

Why does this value matter to you?

Impact reflects the ripple effect of our actions on the world around us. Whether big or small, positive or negative, our impact shapes the lives of others and the environment we inhabit. When we prioritise making a positive impact, we contribute to the wellbeing and collective progress of humanity and the planet. Each moment of empathy and each effort to effect change has the potential to create a lasting legacy that transcends individual existence. By recognising the significance of our impact, we empower ourselves to act with intention, compassion and purpose, fostering a world where every being thrives and flourishes.

4) Community

How do you define this value?

To surround myself with incredible people and contribute to community spirit.

How will you live into this value?

When it is a 'Fuck yes!' then go. Whether it's an event, invitation, breakfast date, go with the fuck yes.

Why does this value matter to you?

Community provides a sense of belonging, support and connection essential for our wellbeing and growth. In community, we find solidarity, shared values and mutual understanding, fostering a sense of unity and belonging. Through collaboration and cooperation within our communities, we amplify our collective strengths, address shared challenges and create opportunities for collective growth and progress. By nurturing and participating in communities, we cultivate meaningful relationships, create a sense of purpose and contribute to a world where every being feels valued, supported and included.

5) Presence

How do you define this value?

To be with reality – what's in and around me, without the need to control or change it.

How will you live into this value?

Name out loud or to myself what is happening around me to bring me right back into the moment.

Why does this value matter to you?

Presence matters because it anchors us in the richness of the moment, allowing us to fully experience life with clarity and awareness. We connect deeply with ourselves, others and the world around us, fostering deeper relationships and a deeper sense of fulfillment. We cultivate mindfulness, resilience and inner peace, empowering ourselves to navigate life's challenges with grace and intention. Presence offers a sanctuary of stillness and connection, inviting us to fully engage with the beauty and wonder of each moment.

Meet Candice

Candice owns a successful PR agency, has two children and is married. Let's just say she is busy! She has support and help around the house as her business takes a lot of time and energy, and she manages a team who look up to her for guidance. She also has clients to attend to, keep happy and PR'd. When she came to me she was ready for a two-week uninterrupted nap. She was living the life she wanted, but had little-to-no time for herself or her husband. It was tag-team time between them to meet their own needs, but when it came time to meet her own, she felt guilty and said she was fine, she didn't need anything anyway. Lies!

Candice's personal life was out of alignment with the pace and rhythm she truly wanted to live at. She had a major client who looked ace on her profile, but who treated her and her team like dirt. This client spoke rudely, hung up before saying goodbye, had unrelenting standards and called non-stop after hours. Candice had an ego problem of saying 'no' which left her feeling suffocated and like she was being used and abused! And she was. But the money this client brought in helped with the mortgage, school fees and adding to the holiday fund. Writing this makes me feel stressed, let alone living it! Candice felt torn whether to let the client go or keep them on for the purpose of 'looking good' and bringing in the cash.

All of it matters, doesn't it? Her purpose, her family, her marriage, money, education. The matters are competing with one another but you can see that 'she' is nowhere to be found in the things that currently matter. Her quality alone time, moving her body, intimacy. She came clean and said, 'Kat, I didn't even want my kids in private schools. My parents said we must and put a lot of pressure on me that I felt I couldn't withstand.' Even though it was mega obvious she should let the problem client go, doing so would mean hustling for new clients. More workload with energy she really didn't have.

It was as clear as day what her next best step was . . . to get back in touch with her core values. If she dropped the pressure of all the things she *should* do and *had* to do and for a moment tapped all the way into herself, her core self who knew what was right, good and true for her, listened to it, wrote it out on paper, then we had a place to begin the real work of reassessing her life with her core values now part of the picture.

Candice valued time, creativity, balance, growth, family (and love). It was time to weave herself and her core values together, look at each area of her life and get very real and honest about what was occupying her time and taking her away from those core values. Her own shit storm was about to begin, but it was a storm worth weathering for the sake of what truly mattered.

Oh, and she did let the client go!

Chapter 13

Fighting the resistance

Egoic resistance is here to stay

As much as we wish it would go away, the relentless force known as 'egoic resistance' ain't going anywhere. As we move ourselves inch by inch or, at times, in quantum leaps towards a self and way of life that feels more true to who we are and who we are becoming, we inevitably encounter moments when our old ways rear their head, casting doubt, fear and uncertainty upon the dreams our hearts have dared to share.

But why does the ego resist when we venture down new pathways, when we dare to challenge our self-made limitations or what others say we cannot do? The answer lies in the very nature of the ego itself – a complex haystack of fears, insecurities and deeply ingrained patterns of thought and behaviour. For the ego, change represents a threat to its carefully constructed identity, a challenge to its sense of control and security. It clings to familiarity like a lifeline, resisting anything that threatens to disrupt the delicate webbing of its perceived reality.

And yet, despite its best efforts to keep us tethered to the known and the familiar, egoic resistance serves a purpose – it's a sign that we're onto something meaningful, something transformative.

It's a signal that we're stepping outside our comfort zone, venturing into unpaved territory where growth and evolution await. It's a reminder that the path to self-realisation is not always easy or straightforward, but one worth pursuing.

So how do we confront and overcome egoic resistance? It begins with awareness – it always does – recognising when the ego is at play, when its whispers of doubt and fear begin to cloud our judgement and dampen our spirits. From there, it's about cultivating a sense of inner strength and resilience – summoning the courage to face our fears, listen to them, love them, and let them know you're going there anyway with unwavering determination and purpose.

But perhaps most importantly, overcoming egoic resistance requires a deep sense of self-trust and self-compassion – a willingness to embrace the uncertainty of the unknown, to forgive ourselves for our perceived shortcomings and to trust in our inherent ability to navigate life's twists and turns with grace and resilience. It's a journey that requires patience, perseverance and a steadfast commitment to our own evolution.

And the winner is . . .

Attaining my personal Olympic gold was no walk in the park. I'd wake up in pain, put my feet on the floor, put the music on, close my eyes, attempt to visualise Free Kat all the while being bombarded with a barrage of seriously unhelpful thoughts.

And damn they were convincing. I dug really fricken deep, remembering what Professor J had told me. I reminded myself, *Kat, it's a twelve-month process, take it day by day.* Each time I visualised my 'free self', I was in an open field among wildflowers.

The sun was out, I was laughing, smiling big, uninhibited, dancing around freely – like bright, Little Kat had done when she was a girl. Damn that vision was powerful. I felt emotional seeing myself in this beautiful, alternate reality. I remembered her. I knew her. She was me. I was her. I *had* to bring her back to life.

When immersed in this vision and feeling, I'd ask myself, *What do I need to do to serve that Kat? How can I bring her back to life?* The answer was: *Move your body and re-engage in your life.* I had no idea who or what was telling me this. Was it god, the universe, or my mind doing a number on me? You bet I struggled with trusting this voice and answer, but it *felt* right. This invisible prescription was to 'Give it everything you've got' and I'd promised myself that I'd trust the process.

Up until then, I'd been avoiding moving my body and going out due to fear of being in pain, so I knew my protective ego was going to give me a run for my money. It was there when I walked to work, on the treadmill, at Pilates, at Zumba class, out at dinner with friends, incessantly saying, *You'll pay for this later, this professor is a nutty one, take those pills, Kat, leave the class, go home now, you won't sleep well, you'll be a bitch to your partner, you'll regret this!*

For ten months I'd been subscribing to my invisible prescription, never missing a day. Feet on floor. Play music. Visualise Free Kat. Do one thing in favour of Future Kat. This was the most committed I had been to doing something that was right, good and true for me. I went from walking, to running, to going on the crosstrainer, to lifting weights, to Zumba, to running a ten-kilometre fun run. Slowly but surely my insides were changing. I was training my mind to act in favour of future Free Kat and my body was following suit. Maybe the nutty professor wasn't so nutty after all.

The first three months had been rough when it came to battling the thoughts in my head; let me tell you, there was nothing pretty or 'love and lighty' about it. But I hadn't let those thoughts take me down, not this fucking time. The more I persisted, the quieter they got. Ten months on, they were still there but weren't as loud. The bass, treble and volume were lower, and I'd found my stride. I'd wake up, plug music in my ears, imagine, feel, act. And yes, I still went to work, cooked and cleaned. It wasn't some at-home retreat where I'd act in favour of my future self all day long. It was one small act within the day. One step at a time.

One day when I was visiting my dad, he asked me, 'How are you going, Neng, you're looking great!' His question made me stop and take a moment to check in with myself. I realised, *Holy shit, I'm not in chronic pain anymore!* I know that sounds wanky but it's true. I was so engrossed and devoted to this practice that I'd naturally gotten myself out of the *Am I in pain? How bad is my pain?* cycle and was in a new cycle of solidifying being a well being.

'Dad, I'm not in pain anymore!' Without even trying or meaning to, I'd lost fifteen kilograms. For the first time in a long time, I was moving my body, not taking any medication and naturally wanting to make better choices for myself. I had a sparkle in my eyes. I was kind to people and patients at work. I could hear myself laugh. Shit, she was here, she wasn't in my future anymore. I was her, she was me. I had got her back. *She* was *here*. I was free from six years of chronic nerve pain. I had emerged from the pits of darkness and was me again. That day, I realised I had become my vision.

What led to me to this point? The willingness to be very real and very honest with myself and my family that I was not okay, that

I needed help, that I wanted something better, something more than a lifelong sentence of chronic pain. That I wanted to be free, to find me again. To know each battle I had faced had required my coping strategies. But in this moment, I had to put aside my old patterns and tell my sophisticated ego stories to pipe down so I could listen to, acknowledge and honour the truth inside – the truth that there was *something more than this.* More to life than pain and suffering. The truth inside was calling for me to live and be authentically me.

Now that I'd claimed my first victory, it inspired more questions about what else was inside me and what other 'gold medals' I could go for. I started to visualise all these intrinsic things: being optimally well, honouring my boundaries, living true to my core values, speaking truth with ease and grace, loving myself and being of service. I would visualise these 'gold medals' and act in favour of them.

This meant certain friendships fell away. I also realised I didn't want to be a nurse anymore. When I gave myself over to being real and honest with myself, my authentic nature took flight and it was as though the forces that be roared with excitement. A new dance was about to begin.

Overcoming egoic resistance

When you state and intend for yourself to know, love and be who you are – and acknowledge this pure desire from the heart by declaring it through journalling, voicing and actions – it gets put out into the world for the forces to work with. But the ego also hears this. And it can respond angrily. It goes through its archives and pulls out the files to remind you that *this* is what happened when you were yourself and how painful that was. *What, we're here again? You really want to do this 'you' thing? You can't, what will people say? How will they react? Imagine what will happen to your relationship? No, no, no, this isn't happening!*

Welcome to the land of resistance. This is the natural egoic response to coming back to and remembering your authentic nature. It's the little yous in there rearing their younger-self heads that locked in certain beliefs and views of the world, others and you, which creates the big old ego. I mean, the ego's job is to protect you, right? So it will go into bat for you in the only way it knows how. Expect resistance to rear its head, barricade the doors to your heart, switch off the power to your dreams and ideas and cut off access to the realm of possibility. The possibility of going after your dream venture, of meeting the person who matches your soul, of making great money doing what you love, of being at ease and relaxed when dating, of whatever it is that's going to make you grow beyond it.

Each time you set an intention you will activate all your junk, all your stuff, and this is what we call resistance. It's like watching a storm come in on your bright, sun-shiny day! Dark clouds and distant showers roll on in. We hear a little rumble in the sky. Soon the blue sky is taken over by Voldemort and his Dementors. The last little glimmer of sun disappears and . . . No, this isn't the moment you fall to your knees. This is the moment you must remember that behind those clouds, *the sun is still shining.* That this is a temporary expected shit storm you need to weather.

As you go on your merry way, taking the next best step towards your authentic self, the ego stories will take one look at this, gather all their evidence from the archives and send up thoughts, feelings and sensations designed to block your flow, have you think, question, second guess, doubt and reconsider if 'this path' is really worth it. Worse yet, whether it's right for you.

Be aware! If you sit in that questioning for too long, your next best steps will lose momentum, eventually causing you to stop and take a trip down 'Same Old Stories Lane'. Soon enough, you'll find yourself making your way back down to ego town, believing the stories and your ego will sigh a sigh of relief, but it's false relief. It's edging you towards a false outcome that has nothing to do with your heart. Which I get; those stories are darn powerful and have created some deep-arse grooves in your neural pathways to convince you that 'this' is where you belong and 'this' is where you shall stay.

Right up to this day (most recently in the lead up to my fabulous, wonderful, amazing wedding), I continue to meet this resistance head-on and find new ways to hose it down. In 2021, I had intended to welcome my feminine nature back into my life. My masculine energy had taken the lead up until this point, pushing, hustling, overworking, proving, as prior to this intention my ego saw no value or point in feminine nature. *What does rest, space, time to be, play or explore achieve?* Sitting on the couch and watching a TV show had to be earnt and god forbid letting anyone else see me rest. If I was resting for a moment and not working, cleaning, washing or pottering, and I heard Steve or the girls coming down the stairs, I'd jump up and 'do' something. Once I became aware of how uncomfortable I was being at rest, I knew deep down it was time to reacquaint myself with a lost part of myself. I knew that when I did this, my authentic nature would grow in presence.

But before all that wonderfulness could emerge, there was a storm to weather, and this one was a long storm. I wanted to claw my way back to the known way, by way of 'doing'. I wanted to take back and occupy the space I had created and fill it with work – work, work, work. My anxiety was at an all-time high and I was stressing about not making money as I had decided to take a nine-month break from coaching. I didn't want to hang out with my friends who owned their own business for fear of appearing 'weak' and felt obliged to justify why I was taking some space and time. The ego can be a real knob sometimes.

For three weeks straight I sat on the bedroom floor right before bed and played 'When You Believe' by Mariah Carey and Whitney Houston, to remind me that all will be well, that all will be okay in time. I had lost sight of why the fuck I had chosen to do this. I considered taking prescribed medication to silence my thoughts. I questioned my faith and trust in the universe and myself. Meditation barely helped, my journal was filled with fear-based thoughts, walking was noisy in my head and working out only gave me an hour's break. Regardless, I kept at it. I was determined to create even the tiniest sliver of space for my authentic nature to peek through if it could. I kept hoping for a break in the clouds where a teeny-tiny bit of blue sky could be seen.

Whenever I managed to catch a breath and moment of clarity before the next wave of anxiety hit, I'd remind myself that I was in the eye of the storm, that this was a normal phase, and if I could just hang on while my ego thrashed us around and surrender to the process, all would (eventually) be well. I had done enough ego-clearing work by now to know that while I was experiencing this shit storm, on the other side of the clouds my intention order was being fulfilled. All I had to do was hold the fuck on and keep the faith in my heart, albeit small, barely alive.

Working with the resistance

So how do we deal with the resistance? How do we manage it and navigate it while simultaneously holding the intention to be who we are? Short answer is, we work *with* it. We don't 'love and light' it, or pretend it doesn't exist. We give it voice, a moment in the spotlight and let it spit the dummy. This is how you neutralise the ego's potency. Shoving it away will keep it in the dark. It will overpower you in the shadows. Spraying love and light spritz will royally piss it off and make you fear its return. So you give it the mic, give it the stage and give it a moment with a shit ton of self-awareness. From the wings, you observe and listen to it, staying as present and aware as you can. But don't stay on watching for too long; after it's vented, cap that ego-mic moment so you don't move into suffering unnecessarily.

Your saving grace in all of this is self-awareness. It always will be. When you notice that you're venturing away from your authentic nature due to the stories in your head projecting themselves onto your reality and you do something about it *before* you start a fight with your partner, or don your fake persona, congratulate yourself. You've realised you're in the thick of navigating your ego resistance with integrity, actively clearing and holding off the Voldemort clouds. Then it's time to choose which tool to pull out of your Mary Poppins bag, apply it and do the work.

You know, just the other morning I woke up in the same house, with the same trees outside, with Bailey and Daisy in my face like they always are in the morning. I walked the same beach as the day before. But I was majorly tangled up in a tsunami of anxiety. My thoughts were so loud that I couldn't even hear them. My head felt like it weighed 100 kilograms and my chest, oh, my chest, my poor chest. It was hard to breathe.

As I walked, I gently rubbed my chest, asked what was going on and said to myself, 'Say it, say it out loud!' But nothing came. So I jumped onto the sand, said 'hi' to the same people I say hi to every day, picked up rubbish like I always do and then unleashed. 'What the fuck, why is life so fucking hard? When will it ever be easy? Why am I such a loser? What the fuck is the fucking point? I'll never be happy, at peace, successful because I'm such a loser! Why do greedy arseholey-type people get rich? Why do they have success? Why do people who don't do the right thing get the same opportunities? What's it going to fucking take for things to be easy? I'm a good person. I do the right thing. I pick up stupid people's rubbish. I help people.' On and on (and on) I went, clearing it all out. It's like an ego-clearing but rather than writing it out on paper, you verbally spray all the gunk out. I felt a bit better.

I came home, cried at my desk, watched myself withdraw and begin my old-style patterned response. I wrote Steve a text message about my current state: *I will do my best to come back to reality and live in reality rather than my story very soon.* I took my youngest bonus daughter Mia shopping with my very grumpy pants on and chose – like, full-blown fucking chose (with every bit of might left in my being) – to come back to my heart, engage from my heart and start again from my true nature: grounded, connected, loving.

Sometimes, well, a lot of the time, nothing is happening in reality – like legit, nothing – yet the stories in your head will warp reality, make you think that *that* is reality and send you into a peaking tailspin. Beautifully complex we are. Might be worth keeping that in mind the next time you're about to let your ego take the steering wheel. In the end, it will only make your day harder than it actually is.

Get this tool in your life: Take Your Meds

And by meds, I mean meditation.

When it comes to meditating I'd like to get real for a second. It is not meant to feel good all the time, be easy all the time, or transcend you all the time. In fact, a lot of the time your thoughts will be gnarly-loud. Very occasionally, you'll have a blissful experience. Either way, meditation your way will keep you in close proximity with the real you, and the watcher of the *not*-you.

My meditation practice changes depending on what is happening in my life. Sometimes I know I need silence. No music. No guidance. No nothing. Just three, six or nine good minutes of silence, where I watch my thoughts, wonder why the hell I am even thinking that and practise being present. Other times I know I need to self-enquire. At the start of a week, I'll pose a question to myself, then spend the remainder of the week meditating upon it. At other times, it looks like Qi Gong, a moving meditation practice that brings me home, quietens the noise and connects me to something intangible but so palpable. These are the practices I've found jam for me and in case you'd like to try them, I've added some details below. I encourage you to find the types of meditation that work for you.

The silent meds

In this practice, I am watching the loudness of my stories. They try to force my focus on what pisses me off about my life, or what I need to get done throughout the day, what I didn't get done yesterday, or if the floors need to be mopped, again. At the same time, I'm being the observer, coming back to the present moment, going back into story, coming back to the present moment, going back into story.

Oops, six minutes is up! I know, it doesn't sound very spiritual, does it? But this is as spiritually real as it gets. Watching, observing, coming back, repeat. Watching, observing, coming back, repeat.

Self-enquiry meds
In this practice, I am seeking answers that will shift my view of life and the way I operate in the world. It deepens the practice of trusting my intuition more and more. And it allows me to follow through on the answers, which keeps self-honour, self-respect and self-confidence alive. It shows my ego that, although I hear you, I hear something else too, and I'm going to follow that nudge, that answer, that guidance that is plugged into my core, the never-lying, all-truth-telling core.

It's the practice of expanding how I've always viewed and done things. If I'm in a place where I feel ready to grow, I write a request like, 'Share with me a truth that I am ready to hear, to feel, to see.' Or if I'm aware that I'm viewing life and going through it with an 'everything is hard' attitude, I write a question like, 'How can I move through my life with greater ease and joy?' Or if I've noticed that my heart is locking down and I'm feeling exasperated with family life, I write a question like, 'What will serve me and my family that I'm currently not in the practice of?' And then, I close my eyes, take deep breaths and let the answers find me. Sometimes those answers find me then and there, and other times they arrive later that day.

Qi Gong
This practice is a standing, slow-moving meditation. Here, I am tapping into the right pace of movement for me, where I'm not trying to control it. It's a matter of feeling into when I'm moving

too fast to 'get this over and done with', or feeling if I'm moving too slow to be more 'Qi Gong' like. Yes, this shit goes through my head. With this 'sensing in', I find the right pace and will say, 'Ah, there it is, there it is.'

Throughout the day when I go about my work, replying to an email, writing books, bonus parenting, cooking meals, cleaning, taking the dogs for a walk, hanging out with Steve or working out, I will often sense if I'm moving 'too fast' or 'too slow' and look for the right pace to settle in and say, 'Ah, there it is.' Qi Gong helps me find the pace and rhythm that is right, good and true for me and the situation.

Meet Liv

When your ego stories are loud and seem so real that you think they're the whole truth and nothing but the truth so help you god, then please use this exercise. I have little black books dedicated to clearing out the mess in my head. If anyone ever gets a hold of them, I promise I'm okay, but I do have to warn you, they're dark. Like really dark. And that's okay – the whole point of this process is to get the ego-darkness out from inside and scare it with the light of day. I call this the Ego Clearing exercise, and here's how it worked for my dear client (now a dear friend) Liv.

Liv sent me this email in 2020:

Dear Kat,

I have no idea what I want or need, I just know that you are the right person to talk to.

I have confronted, and then avoided, and then confronted, and then denied that the work needs to be done – and it has come to a point that

I just need to fkn deal with whatever is going on in my head, heart and body in regard to relationships.

Iso has been the actual best, in that it has allowed me the space to do the work and hear what is really coming up for me. I have really used this time to dig as deep as I can possibly go by myself to uncover every-thing within my power that causes me to be the way that I am and have identified a number of things. I have journalled, I have burnt shit in the new moon, I have done sacral chakra healing – woo-woo you name it, I've done it.

But what really resonated with me and gave me hope was your story with Steve – I feel there may be something in this that will enable you to help me unlock another part of the many walls I have seemingly put up.

HELLLLLLLLLP MEEEEEEEEEE PLEEEEASE.

Liv

In our first session, I took Liv through the Ego Clearing tool and introduced her to the practice of giving her ego a voice and airtime, but with structure, framework, an end point and a way to move beyond it. It's a process of deconstructing the giant invisible monster that lives in our head.

Bonus tool: Ego Clearing

Using the Ego Clearing tool, first, you zoom *into* the ego's per-spective and how it views your relationship, your interactions, what you do and what you don't do. Here, you're giving it a chance to chuck a wobbly without interrupting it with love, light or logic. When you do this exercise, for the first part, there is no loving logic – only the ego's version of what it believes to be right and wrong. When we come to the end of the exercise, then it's time to zoom *out* and apply the work that will tap into greater perspective, greater truth and answers that are there to serve you at the deepest level.

You've already got self-awareness present while you do this exercise, and now that you've given your ego and its stories the metaphorical stage and mic, you connect back to what matters: the bigger picture. Create the space to get quiet, enquire and journal, to remind yourself of your core values and where you're headed in terms of your heart's result, which in Liv's case was to have a connected and real relationship. Imagine yourself living and breathing in that bigger picture, zoomed out from the ego's tight view of whatever situation you're stuck in. From this place ask: what is your next best step, to serve what your heart seeks? From this quiet space, reflect on the following questions – let the answers find you. Here's the exercise in practice with Liv:

What is the situation (neutral)?
- I (Liv) want to be my true self and own who I am in a loving, caring relationship.

What is the current reality (present)?
- Single.

What is your current approach to relationships?
- I see a guy I am interested in and then think to myself that he's out of my league and tell one of my friends to get with them.
- Friend-zone them.
- Don't tell them how I am feeling or what I want.
- Go with their flow and never say what I'd like or not like.

- Keep a lot inside to 'play it cool'.
- Set big expectations without telling them and then get gravely disappointed when the expectations/plans I had in my head don't go to plan.

What are your current thoughts about the situation (charged)?
- Why do I miss out?
- Why can't I be picked?
- What do they (other women) have that I don't?
- What do I have to do to be chosen?
- What's wrong with me?
- What am I missing? What am I not doing?
- I'm not chosen because I'm not skinny.
- When will it be my turn?
- There's no hope. I'll be single forever.

What are your feelings about the situation (charged)?
- Angry, sad, hurt, frustrated, pathetic, embarrassed.

What is your usual coping strategy (reaction)?
- Friend-zone guys quickly.
- Pretend I'm not that interested.
- Don't let on that I am hurt.
- Play it cool.
- Make work the priority.

What are you making it mean about you (personalising)?
- I am not worth choosing (Enneagram #2 The Helper).

What are you making it mean about others (comparing)?

- How come they get to be loved? What are they doing that I'm not?

What are you making it mean about life (catastrophising)?

- Life's unfair. What do I have to do to get life to notice me?

What is the inevitable outcome?

- I'll focus on my work.
- I'll pretend I don't want this.
- I'll tell people it's not important to me.
- I'll lie to myself that I am okay.
- I'll wait. I'll settle. I'll be alone.

What is your next best step?

- To state out loud what *I* want and to communicate with the person I am seeing how I feel, aka be vulnerable.

Now, three years later, Ms Liv has given birth to her first baby, Rose, with her partner by her side, loving her and doing life with her. It didn't come without a lot of work, a lot of reminding herself to return home to herself and a lot of navigating of ego resistance. When she met her partner, she felt very challenged to speak up, to say that she cared for him, liked him, even loved him. She said, 'Yeah, I've let him know I care', to which I replied, 'But have you said the words with your heart, into his eyes?'

Liv had to clear her ego many times before she could say what her heart wanted to say, so she could stay true to her authentic self and not play into her Enneagram persona, leading down the slippery slide which lands in average levels of personal development and behaviour. She made her bigger result matter, her truth matter, and shifted her ego's focus of 'please pick me' to sharing herself openly, honestly and authentically.

I received this text message from Liv in April 2023:

My Katty,

I feel most emotionally excited sharing this with you above anyone else in my life.

Because without you, this journey wouldn't exist.

I know I have told you before, but I truly think about you every second of the day and how grateful I am for this life that you helped me see was for me.

Thank you will never be enough.

Attached was an image of her sonogram.

Yep, I'm crying too.

Chapter 14

Connecting to others

Next-level relationships

Getting real and honest with how you're showing up, doing life and operating in the world means you're willing change to enter your life. When I got real and honest with how I was showing up, I was then able to get real and honest with what was required (the next best step) to show up as the *real* me.

Because of that, I overcame chronic pain, ended a co-dependent relationship, started dating myself (and started actually kinda liking me), relied on my inner compass to guide my own life, left nursing, started a business, tended to my relationship with money and sex, met Steve, created a solid family unit with Steve, created an epic community (that's you), and called in like-minded souls to jam with, sit with, cry with, laugh with and do life with. Each of these experiences challenged me to dig in deep, reach inside all parts of me, untangle myself and come out with the truth beating in my heart. I'd like to extend that challenge – and its rich rewards – to you too.

Two people who are willing to walk the path of authenticity is a next-level challenge for your relationship, but the rewards are so worth it. Add to that parenting or bonus parenting and you build yourself one hell of an epic family. Steve and I work towards big picture end results across three levels: as individuals, as a couple, and as a family. Each of these calls upon our core values: to live into the vision we hold, to enquire and reflect, and to take the next best step to serve this vision. We made a pact in the beginning to be responsible and accountable for our mental, emotional, physical and spiritual wellbeing. We said we're not each other's parents when it comes to always 'pulling the other one up', but that we both have permission to let the other know when it's time to take greater responsibility when shit starts to get wobbly.

Being a bonus parent has been an invitation to up my game in the authenticity arena. There are now two little girls (not so little now, unlike when I met them at ages nine and seven), who are watching, noticing and observing. My actions, what I say, how I show up and everything in between is 'seen'. Now I have so many more reasons than just 'me' to keep showing up for this work.

It's hard at times, but so worth it

When I met Steve and became a bonus parent, it was 'batter up, buttercup'. It was time to step into the arena again, get my arse kicked, face my shadows, integrate them, retrieve lost selves, manage a new angle of ego stories and emerge from deep waters with even more 'me'. I lost myself a little, my footing, my grounding. All of a sudden I was in relationship with Steve, the two girls and all that came with a split family. *How do I act? How do I be? Where's the line to not cross? What's my place? What's my role? Who the fuck am I in all this?* I was in a spin.

The level of realness, honesty, responsibility and accountability required to face and own my shit so I could show up as a bonus parent with my real self intact and be an example of a human I was proud of, was not a level I was prepared for. I went in naive, simply happy to be in love with Steve and face whatever came with that love. 'Happy' is an interesting way to describe it. My ego stories flared, my obsessive-compulsive tendencies rose, my persona and its need to escape reality and control my reality was in full flight.

I was drowning in trying to do the 'right' thing. Trying to figure out the 'right way' to navigate this new land and territory so I wouldn't upset anyone, step on anyone's toes and to not be the 'bad guy', so I wouldn't get kicked out and feel rejected. This was, of course, my default way of going about it. But being so busy figuring out the 'right way' didn't draw me closer to the family, it kept me apart. It created distance between us which was keeping my ego stories very lit and alive in their quest to keep me 'safe'. Safe from rejection. Safe from abandonment. Safe from the 'you're not my real mum' comment, which to be honest has only been said once to my face. But what was I missing out on? Deep connection, togetherness, love.

Knowing which is authentic you and ego-persona you matters and is a life changer. For me, it quite literally saves me from leaving my relationship with Steve. I can talk about leaving Steve, even to his face, knowing where it's coming from, and he does too. In my truth, I know all the way down to my core that Steve is my love. He is not only a rock, he's a giant boulder who supports me to no end and cheers me on as if he has pom-poms in his hands shouting, 'Give me a K, give me an A, give me a T!' No conversation is off limits. We are lovingly and radically honest, and we are a damn good team.

One of my greatest heart's desires was to be in a relationship that was deeply fulfilling, solid, fun and loving. One of my greatest fears was that I was unloveable – too broken, too damaged, too much. So to move towards and into a relationship with Steve, who is loving, solid, fun, dependable, caring, thoughtful, open, honest, supportive and all the bloody things, really messed with my fears and limiting beliefs. He loves me in my pitch-black darkness, in my blinding light and in all my colours in between. That right there is the kryptonite to my ego stories, and so my ego tries to find reasons to leave, why we don't work and why we're not compatible.

Steve's not conscious enough, not sensitive enough, he doesn't get me, he doesn't know how to hold me, he doesn't understand me. My ego stories run this over and over, project it onto my reality and look for an 'out' anywhere they can. My ego seeks to be alone because that's where I'm 'safest'. It's Enneagram #4 The Individualist at work, operating at the average level of development. If I identify with that story without any connection to my authentic self, I'll be walking from my relationship and heading towards my castle built for one (animals welcome).

This is why it matters.

You might be thinking of ending a relationship that has its challenges, but has so much love, depth and real care there. You might be staying in a relationship with someone who diminishes your soul, your spark, your heart. You might be applying for jobs that appeal to your ego self, while ignoring what truly lights you up. You might be arguing over total bullshit with your partner, thinking you're right and that more arguing will get them to concede. You might be capping your earning potential and settling for the story 'this is all I'm worth'. You might be living in accordance with your family's principles and disregarding what feels right for you. You might be marrying someone you know in your core is not for you.

It matters because two very different lives and realities can and will be created, depending on which self you give the most airtime. It matters because you might end a relationship that requires you to go deeper, look deeper and be vulnerable. It matters because you might stay in a relationship that eats your shine for breakfast, lunch and dinner. It matters because you might spend sixty hours a week working and grinding in a place that is terribly misaligned for you. It matters because there is growth, possibility and potential in walking the path of your authentic self.

Now, if Steve were a total knob who treated me poorly, was disengaged from the relationship and himself, who was identified strongly with his own ego and persona, who gaslit me, called me a psycho or hormonal, who promised he would change and never did, who sat on his arse and expected me to wait on him, who spoke to me harshly, condescendingly and yet seemed to speak to everyone else like a non-jerk, then I'd walk. But in my reality, Steve's the giant boulder. It's just in my ego story that he's a threat. He's a threat to my ego's quest to go it alone.

This is why it matters to come back home to our authentic nature and to know the difference between our ego-projected stories and our actual truth. Doing so takes a shit ton of observation, zooming out, mining your thoughts and being curious about where your intentions are coming from. It really is a full-time job. There'll be days you'll want to call in sick. You'll want to drop down to part-time or become a contractor who comes in and out as you please. Or you'll want to quit altogether. The choice, at the end of the day, is indeed yours. Just be willing to own how you and your life pans out as a result.

Who is your outer brat protecting?

When Steve and I first got together, my ego stuff threw a spanner in the works. It was not a fan of Steve being solid, grounded, loving, caring, faithful, emotionally available, communicative and all the rest. Even though this is what I asked for from my heart, this new reality did not match my old stories and old reality. So I returned to patterns of closing off, shutting down, not speaking up, withholding, saying 'Yep, I'm fine' when I for sure was not fine and something was on my chest to speak out loud.

One afternoon, Steve said, 'I thought I was dating a woman, not a child. This is a relationship out of want, not need, so do what you gotta do to be the woman I know you are.'

Holy shitballs. My ego crawled under a rock and hid, and I was left with nothing but truth and the invitation to be real and honest with myself. Steve having his values intact and holding bigger-picture intentions in the forefront of his mind and heart, along with his willingness to be real and honest with me, meant it was time to rise the fuck up, accept my new reality, enjoy my new reality, and be me in this relationship. But first, I needed to tend to the wounded part in me that was trying to prove my 'I don't need a man, I'm Little Miss Inde-fucking-pendent', who was thrashing around inside, playing out the same patterns and operating in my average health of Enneagram #4.

It was thirteen-year-old Kat, the one who had been in the world long enough to know that people didn't always have the best intentions. The one who believed that people might say they're there for you but really, they're not. That people might say they'll listen to you, but they don't. The pimple-faced, angry, broken, self-loathing teenager who wanted to prove to the world that, 'I don't need you or anybody!' Before I could show up as a better version of myself, I needed to tend to her, listen to her, love her and expand her locked-in way of seeing life. If I didn't, she'd watch me try to do better, swipe me at the knees and replay the pattern.

Getting to the truth of what's going on

My eldest bonus daughter, Ally, and I went through a tough period. Real tough. We were in an energetic war with one another. I can't tell you the amount of times I wanted to leave the family home, call it quits and let them be. At that stage, Ally felt that I was the problem, the reason her dad didn't love her anymore. All of our egos stomped around the house trying to gain control and 'work it out'. Problem was, we were trying to work it out *cognitively* and with our sophisticated stories in charge. I remember sitting on the couch crying, saying to Steve, 'Please, the easiest thing here is for me to leave, so you can both have your relationship back.' It had been almost two years of this battle and I was downright exhausted. Ego said, 'You're the problem, *Expelliarmus!*'

A few days later, I took a walk along the beach, which is when I have chats with the forces of nature. I said, 'Please, show me the truth of this matter' and walked as I stayed open for an answer to find me. Two women having a conversation passed by. One of them said, 'This isn't about you, this is about them.' Those words went straight past my mind and into my heart. I sighed a breath of relief and a tear rolled down my cheek. The answers kept coming in, letting me know that the real healing needed to happen between Steve and his daughter, that he had been withholding from their relationship due to her difficult shift from being a little girl to a teenager.

In that moment it became clear that we were stuck in a pattern of defending our stories in ego town. Steve's ego was making Ally feel that his love was conditional because she was acting up, her ego blamed me for him not loving her, and my ego was making me the problem, making me want to run. But that walk, oh that life-changing walk, coupled with a question, coupled with space for the answer to arrive, led to truth.

I shared this with Steve and his heart felt the resonance. He could see it all. He called his daughter, picked her up and the two of them walked for almost two hours. He said, 'We have both made our relationship the way it is, and it's up to us to bring it back. This has nothing to do with Kat, it's just about you and me. Share with me all the things that are on your mind, in your heart and what you're upset about.'

She was a little unsure if she could and Steve reiterated, 'I am here to listen, not defend.' She spoke, and spoke, and spoke and Steve kept saying, 'Okay, and what else?', giving her the space to clear much of what was inside of her without making her wrong. Then, they made a pact to repair their relationship. To make time for one another, to have 'just them' time. I'd say it took around six weeks for trust to build, for awkwardness to not be there and for her to move back into our home. The stronger she and Steve got, the stronger she and I got. We could go back to being 'us' because she felt the love from her dad.

All our egos crawled under a rock and we were left with nothing but truth and the invitation to be real and honest with one another. For me, the truth meant I didn't need to run away and be alone forever (damn it, says ego). For Steve, the truth meant his heart was ready to open and expand. For Ally, it meant she wasn't unloved and replaced. The distinction between ego stories and our truth leads to completely different destinations, as you can see from our experience. New realities are possible if we are prepared to know who we're not, know who we are, and mine our thoughts for the truth. These days, Steve and Ally are two tight peas in a pod and Ally and I are the best we've ever been. In an alternate reality, well, there would have been a lot of pain, disconnection and staying in keeping the story alive.

Get this tool into your life: My Story

The stories we keep hashing and rehashing have immense power over how we see reality. Instead of seeing and experiencing reality for what it is, we view it through our stories, which are often a smoky haze. Instead of dealing with reality as it is, we deal with it through the lens of our pain, our wounds, our junk, our stuff and reality never, or rarely, is faced. We're fighting what we *think* is happening rather than getting close to what actually *is*.

Popping the 'story bubble' can be scary, I know, because it means you're on the verge of being real and honest with what is actually there for you to see, feel, hear and experience. This is why knowing what story you're keeping alive matters.

What story are *you* keeping alive?

For what purpose are you keeping it alive? What 'kink' does your ego get out of it?

What is it keeping you 'safe' from?

How is this story *really* affecting you, if you were real and honest with yourself?

What part of you needs to be seen, held, heard, loved and expanded to move on from this story?

Meet Steve and me

Since this chapter is all about relationships and because we have a regular segment on my podcast about relationships, I thought why not share how Steve and I do the work, because let's face it, we ain't perfect. We get on each other's nerves and know each other's sore spots and, at times, press them.

When Steve and I first got together, we made an agreement that we were choosing our relationship out of want, not out of need. We'd done a lot of work on ourselves as individuals and wanted to set out from the get-go that we were both independent *and* inter-dependent. We also agreed on how we'd love our relationship to be by doing an exercise that helped us get very clear on what we wanted the overall energy and feel to be, what we each would do to contribute to that and how we'd approach one another when the other wasn't stepping up.

The exercise required us to be radically honest. I mean, it could have been the end of us if we'd wanted wildly different things. We spoke about this but went through with it anyway and I tell you, it's something we continue to come back to. As I write this, we are two weeks away from getting married, something that we planned to do in 2020 but some big germ decided to shut down the whole planet (lucky Mother Earth). We've been irritable with one another, more than we've ever been. Our tone has been sharper, our fuses have been shorter and it's almost as though we're looking to be offended by each other. That kind of behaviour followed by clearing our egos, resetting, re-engaging and then back to sharp tones, short fuses and 'I didn't say that', or, 'well, I didn't mean it like that' has been utterly exhausting.

Thank the heavens I had a kinesiology appointment booked.

As it turned out, my irritability pot was being stirred by Little Miss Independent Kat, the one who 'didn't need no one'. Deep in my story I've been afraid of being trapped, fearing that 'there's no way out if I marry him'. My fears want to run, or at the very least have an exit strategy or to know where the door is. My heart says, 'You're okay, darling.'

Bonus tool: What We *Really* Want?

When Steve and I really need to work through our stuff, we use a tool we call What We *Really* Want? Important note: this is a tool to do with your *current* person. Together. Not one of you deciding how it's going to be and not one of you saying, 'I don't care, you do it for us'. Dual responsibility. Answer the following questions (our answers are below, as an example):

What's the overall energy of our relationship?
• Caring, light-hearted, real, trusting, free, deep love, playful, safe space.

What are we willing do to contribute to it?
• Communicate kindly, gently, with radical honesty.
• Once a month Scenic Sundays.
• Touch, hold hands, regular intimacy, affection, kisses hello and goodbye and good morning.
• Each live our own lives – nurture friendships together and also apart, fulfill our own desires and interests independently.
• Commit to continuing our mental, emotional, spiritual and physical growth and development.

What are the no-go zones?

- Putting the other down around others for a laugh.
- In heated conversations, no swearing to be used to put the other person down like 'you fucking idiot'.
- Infidelity.
- Withholding love as a punishment.
- Manipulating, gaslighting, controlling the other.
- *Any* form of abuse.

When we are out of alignment with this result, what will we do about it?

- Communicate, even (and especially) when it's hard.
- Get out of the house (neutral environment) to clear our frustrations – take a walk so we're next to one another and not at home where doors can be slammed.
- Get very clear on where our egos are getting involved and what is actual truth.
- Frame sentences with 'my ego says' or 'my truth knows'.
- Listen without interrupting the other.
- Nothing gets left off the table. It's all out.

It seems simple, but most answers to the shit that goes down in our lives are painfully simple. I know when I (my ego) is looking for a fight with Steve. I can feel it bubbling away inside, creating very convincing narratives as to why it's okay to shut off, close my heart and give him the silent treatment. Or why it's okay to speak abruptly to him with little regard for how it might make him feel. I watch how I'm behaving, my body language and what I start focusing on. There's always the observer observing, but sometimes, I pretend I can't see what I'm doing.

Sometimes I can break free from my ego's grip and reorientate myself back to my true nature. Other times, well, it's on like Donkey Kong. Usually it's when I'm tired, have kept important matters bottled up, or when I feel shit about myself. Except, Steve is also on his own path of personal and spiritual development. He too knows his ego and his true nature, so to be real, it's pretty rare when both our egos get to have a romper stomper of an argument.

We were on our way to my friend's wedding and Steve said he wanted me to come to an appointment with little notice and no option other than to say 'yes'. I looked at my diary and had coaching clients and meetings, so I said to choose another date. Steve's authentic self said farewell for a moment, and mine was about to bid me farewell too. His ego took over and went through all the times he'd supported me (his pattern) when I'd asked him to and how I was selfish, never had his back and that I took him for granted. Well, that hit a nerve. My ego went on to remind him that he had no right to tell me what to do and reeled off all the things that I did to support him and our family, which *he* took for granted.

Silence.

Great Walls of China built around our hearts.

Heads pounding.

Bodies closed off.

Stories like 'Go fuck yourself!' playing in our heads.

What was really going on was that Steve's wound of being unsupported and my wound of being controlled reared their heads simultaneously. Those two forces went to town on each other and in that moment of silence, I remembered our agreement. I spoke calmly and shared what this argument was really about. He agreed. Our authentic selves came back into the car within minutes and we communicated openly, honestly and gave one another the opportunity to have the same conversation but with way more presence.

Our original agreement keeps us in check and in alignment with our hearts. Steve will look at me and say, 'I know your ego is looking for a fight and it ain't gonna get one,' or he'll smoosh my cheeks and say, 'You're so cute'. While my ego finds this incredibly infuriating, it disarms me and I remind myself that I neither need nor want to fight.

In that moment he is staying true to his authentic self and our agreement and I can feel that. When he doesn't engage I kinda feel like an idiot. I'm the one being petty, petulant and pouty while he's singing in the kitchen, going about his day unbothered.

Shame bathing. Guilt. Set the high standard to 'never do that again'. But you will, and that's okay.

Chapter 15

Staying true

Breaking the pattern

When I first started my quest for 'the real Kat' back in my twenties, I felt like Dorothy from *The Wizard of Oz* stepping onto the yellow brick road for the first time. I was like, 'Hell to the yeah, as soon as I find "me", all my shit will be sorted and my life will be amazing. Let's do this!' Like Dorothy, I thought my problems would be solved the minute I found my guru with all the answers. Turns out, we both went on a long-arse gnarly journey only to be told we had the solution to our problems inside us all along.

Does this new reality have zero problems? No.

Does this new reality have zero people who will trigger you? No.

Does this new reality mean that all your shit from the past vanishes and you're squeaky-clean healed? No.

Does this new reality have zero ego, stories and personas? No.

Does this new reality promise authentic you and authentic living all the time? No.

Soz.

You will continue to create problems and experience problems. Your family will still trigger you. Your tender wounds from the past will remind you *this is not safe* and bring about your default coping strategies and resistance to reality. Your ego, its stories and exhausting personas will be ready and waiting to hijack you. You will default into old, patterned ways.

Story time is done, princess

In my previous life I hated me. I was riddled with chronic pain and on pain medication every day. I relied on my boyfriend to feel safe. I couldn't spend a quiet moment with myself, let alone dare to believe that I could do the work I'm doing today. I took drugs and alcohol to escape reality, dated guys without even checking in with myself if I liked them, and drove myself into the ground more times than I care to think about. I threw up my food, drank skinny-me teas until I was fifty kilograms and still thought I was fat. I was the definition of 'not okay'.

But there's that old saying, 'The grass is greener where you water it', and I had been watering all the weeds and expecting a rose to grow. That right there is accountability and responsibility working its magic, asking us to level-the-fuck-up, buttercup! So I did and things got better, and I continue doing the work day after day after day. Will it ever stop? No. Has it got better? Yes. Better enough to ever stop the work? No. It never ends . . . So why, I hear you ask, do we bother with this new way forward? Why do the work to come back home to ourselves when none of the shit stuff goes away?

That's the red pill from *The Matrix* that you and I are swallowing. It doesn't go away and life itself doesn't get easier . . . but by living authentically, the way you navigate it does. The rapidness of coming back to yourself, your values, your quiet space, your practices is available to you. You'll come up for air more often and breathe in that air a little longer each time, and when your ego stories come back, you'll know that it's just that, stories. You'll know that it's not authentic you. It's an all-knowing. An indescribable feeling of trust that you're plugged into *you*, all the way deep down inside. You don't know *how* you know, but you do. You don't know how you know what you *need*, but you do. You don't know how you know what to *do*, but you do. You have no idea how all of you connects and communicates, but it does. And no one, not even yourself, can take it from you. That, I promise. You will protect and honour this newfound way because you simply cannot, any longer, align and identify with what you *thought* was real.

I remember when I was twenty-seven, pulling over on the side of the road and ringing a friend, Ava. I'd been hitting my head with my hand to make the thoughts stop. On repeat they were telling me, *I hate you, I hate you, I hate you. You're worthless. You're of no value. You're a waste of space.*

I was so attached to these thoughts that the pain in my head was real. I wanted to die. I wanted out. I wanted to press the 'abort life's mission' button and ascend far, far away from planet Earth. I had no space between the real me and these thoughts. I was the thoughts. I was the ego. I was the story.

I saw no light, no hope, no new way. In my mind, I was doomed to suffer. But thank goodness I used, and still do, my inherited stubbornness to get myself the fuck out of my own way. Just like I did when I got myself out of chronic pain, I said, 'Alright, Ms John, there's no checking out until you've given this a red-hot crack! You're not extra fucked up. In fact, I think this ego business loves thinking that "we are" extra fucked up so we can stay in victimhood, stay in woe is me, stay in not being empowered.'

Well, story time is done, princess.

Why being authentic is worth it

Think of the big stuff you've overcome. Heartbreak, burnout, diseases, the loss of a loved one (fur babies included) and how you thought there was no fricken way you'd be coming out of that blackness. That there was no way out of the deep-arse pit of doom. But, in time, there was. And mixed with time was support, getting help, patience, trust, faith, walking, journalling, rest, sleep, dancing, screaming into pillows and crying. In time, this period will add to the 'big stuff' you've overcome, and there will come a moment where you will have shifted most of the weight from inauthenticity to authenticity, fake to real, insincere to honest.

You will have rough-as-guts moments. You will spiral. You will align with your ego, again and again. You will forget who you are. You will question who the fuck you are. You will doubt if who you are is in fact who you are. You will feel awkward around some people. You will attempt to play it small, overpower, be perfect, overachieve, overnice, control – the burger with the lot. And that is all groovy. That is all good. That is all normal. That is accepting the human mother-fucking experience.

What I can promise you is this. You will have all the reasons and stories in the world to abandon yourself and whack some false version of you on. That mask will want to be worn at school pick-up, when you go on dates, when you go for that job interview, when you tell your partner that everything is 'fine', and when you tell yourself that everything is 'fine'. But with the knowledge and tools you've gained through this book, you now have greater choice and agency over these stories. And this means you now have *real* choice in your life, moment to moment, to assess and enquire if the real you is present or not.

You'll have real, honest and enriching relationships

Your willingness to be real with yourself allows you to be real with others. Your willingness to swallow your pride, put ego aside, apologise and admit where you were being closed-minded is invaluable to creating trust in relationships.

I was at our local grocer one afternoon with my youngest bonus daughter, Mia. That week I was up to my eyeballs in overwhelm as the girls had moved in with us. My persona took over and my way to survive was to close my energy down so I could get on with doing what had to be done around the house, while holding space for the girls, trying to coordinate with Steve, and tending to my work.

We were walking down the aisle and I turned to Mia and said, 'I know I've been distant and not myself this past week, and I'm sorry for that. You gotta know it's not you. I'm overwhelmed and trying to figure this out and adapt to the change. I've never been a full-time bonus parent before.'

She said, 'Kitty, I get it. It must be a big change for you. Tell me how I can help you.'

I grabbed her in a loving headlock and hugged her. Boom. Authenticity land. Real-conversation land. Honest land. Out-of-persona land. In-truth land. Staying on the trajectory of withholding my energy, 'doing the do' and getting shit done would have led to further disconnection, resentment, awkwardness and the rest. I get that eating responsibility and accountability isn't the most pleasant meal, but damn it feels good once you own your stuff.

As I cooked dinner that night Mia asked, 'Kitty, want me to put the washing on?'

You'll be a well being

When your thoughts and actions are synced, you're free from the friction caused by working against your grain. You're not bogged down by thinking of having a smoke, or recovering from another bender, or making yourself feel guilty for drinking a bottle of wine each night, or eating shit food that makes you feel heavy, bloated and blurrgh. You'll naturally want to take better care of yourself because you value vibrancy, life force, movement, energy and feeling well. You'll create better sleep hygiene, phone boundaries, relationships with food and eating, and spend more time taking care of yourself, balanced with a few times here and there eating your 'naughty' foods, staying up late, or whatever.

To contribute to being a well being I do a stack of little things that all add up to 'I feel good!' The one that is most important to my mental health is to not touch my phone in the morning. It's been a practice for some time but the ego maniac dopamine junkie in my brain wants to see who 'loves me', 'likes me', 'commented on me'. Ugh, so me-monster vibes. I refuse to give in to it. I don't open my phone until I have cuddles with Steve, smooch Bailey and Daisy, walk on the beach and do my three good minutes of something good. No 'love' or 'like' or 'comment' means more than protecting my wellbeing.

Coming back to yourself means you are prepared to listen to what's right, good and true for you as the human you are today and the future self who's calling you forward. That might mean having a chat with your friends and letting them know why you're driving instead of drinking or having two drinks instead of ten. That might mean letting your family know about the food changes you're making, that you'd love their support and to not make fun of you. That might mean having a slightly different bed routine to your partner, because you want to go to bed without screens. But can I also say that it doesn't mean you need to be inflexibly rigid, wound-up and uptight about your 'what's right, good and true for you'. There are extreme ends of the spectrum but we're looking for the sweet spot between them.

I've done all of the above and my friends still love me. Steve and I are still together. And all the while, I'm intact. Knowing what's good for you helps you to communicate to the people around you what matters, why it matters and that you'd love their understanding. And in the same breath, give them a moment of grace to catch up with you.

You'll have greater purpose

To have some 'thing' matter to us is for that 'thing' to mean something of importance, of significance. For something to be important it needs to be something we value. When you come back home to yourself, there is greater desire and capacity to be dedicated to passions that light you up. There is less time spent (wasted) on bullshit fighting with friends or your partner, less time spent (wasted) recovering from hangovers, less time spent (wasted) bitching about the state of the world and the shit leaders in charge. Why? Because you'll be living closely to your true and authentic way, which means you'll nip pesky problems or misunderstandings in the bud. You won't want to spend the whole day or week thinking about how annoyed you are and staying in story. You'll consider how you want to spend your Sunday, either feeling fresh or foggy. You'll be spending time on what genuinely inspires you. That clean, clear energy propels you forward and keeps you on path and on purpose.

Mia was keen to work and earn money. I suggested she look to combine what she loved with being paid for it. She loves animals and playing sport. We offered to help put a post on our local Facebook group offering to walk people's dogs. In an instant we received a message, met a couple of dog owners and she was walking their pup two days later. Steve and I watched her come home from school, ride her bike to the dog owner's house, walk the doggy and ride home three to four times a week. She was beaming. She felt so good in herself, proud and on purpose. She told me, 'Kitty, I don't even miss being on my phone because I love this feeling so much. I feel like I have purpose.'

When our authentic selves are living, breathing and present in our lives, the invisible feelings we long to feel are also living, breathing and present. Self-respect, self-love, self-honour, self-worth and self-confidence start to bubble away inside of us and when we fill up on that, it spills out and touches the lives of others. People will say, 'You seem happy' or, 'You look different, did you change your hair?' or, 'Wow, you seem really solid!' These invisible yet palpable feelings help us stand rooted in who we are. They help us feel genuinely proud of who we are. This goodness continues to feed what matters, which contributes to more goodness, which spreads goodness out into the world. A cycle to nurture.

Authenticity matters because it brings us back to our core self, our innate sense of what is right for us, good for us and true for us. It plugs us into our power, our intentions that are rooted in our hearts, and grounds us in making choices where we and others are considered with care and integrity. If we don't see how important knowing and being our authentic self is, then good luck to humanity. Good luck to the future generations and what they will endure. Good luck to the future of some of our species.

Let's not wish the future good luck and instead, get to work on what matters.

You'll lead by example

I mean, we all know we need this more than ever, but if we wait for the day where people in positions of power come into their authentic selves, we might not live to tell the tale! If you're like me, you probably wonder how the hell they got into power and what kind of world we live in that allows such people to be making worldly decisions.

In 2014, I went to Cambodia with a Rotary program called World of Difference. Alongside bringing certain villages their requested needs, we were shown a place I'll never forget: the Killing Fields. In the 1970s, Cambodian leader Pol Pot advocated a radical Communist revolution that would wipe out Western influences. Some 1.5 to 2 million people were killed. How this happened, I cannot fathom. How this still happens in other places around the world, I cannot believe. How deeply entrenched and identified with their egos some must be, to think that killing certain kinds of humans is the answer. I stand by the idea that discerning between genuine truth, and ego truth, and choosing to live in accordance with genuine truth, is an almighty key to change.

We cannot wait for our current leaders to be the examples we want them to be. We need to be the leaders of our own lives, our own families, our own relationships and interactions with fellow humans. Be it, live it, exemplify it. Anthropologist Margaret Mead said, 'Never doubt that a small group of thoughtful, committed citizens can change the world; indeed, it's the only thing that ever has.'

Steve and I watch our neighbours, Greg and Tracy, run their Elwood Sourdough bread shop from their garage. They're on the corner of the canal where, each morning, music is played with yummy bread displayed alongside warm smiles. They know people by name. They take a moment to chat. They say hello even if you're not buying bread. They sit on the bridge of the canal having a cuppa, chatting, watching the sun go down. They are caretakers of the canal and are in communication with the council to have our waterways cleaned up. They are an example of community spirit and #relationshipgoals. Have you met people like that? People who are good humans, but not good humans as a strategy, just good, solid, kind people making the world a better place by firstly, being themselves, and secondly, sharing themselves generously.

Instead of waiting for world leaders to set the example, be an example in the world. That's how each of us contributes to changing it for the better. Start by asking, 'How do I want to be remembered? If my time were up tomorrow, what message, legacy or imprint would I want to leave? What mark would I want to leave on someone's heart?'

For humanity
John Lennon, the legend, wrote the most amazing lyrics to 'Imagine' which we know all too well. Call me crazy, a dreamer, a wishful thinker, but in my pure heart, I see a new reality.

Eckhart Tolle's book, *A New Earth*, describes how our attachment to the ego creates the dysfunction that leads to anger, jealousy and unhappiness. He shows readers how to awaken to a new state of consciousness and follow the path to a truly fulfilling existence. I know that I'm not the only 'crazy, dreamer, wishful thinker'! Within yourself, I'm sure that you too can see the potential of us as a species.

That real shift could take place if we changed the way we schooled children, and the curriculum, taught from such a young and tender age. If we are sponges between the ages of zero and seven years old, imagine if, at day-care, kindergarten, pre-school and primary school, the curriculum fuelled kids with the foundations of ethical philosophy. Imagine classes that supported them in being themselves, celebrating others, how to handle the ego or the 'dark voice' as I describe it to my bonus daughters, and choose the 'light voice' or truth instead. Imagine classes about values, taking care of one another, how to handle big emotions, how to navigate conflict and disagreements, how to celebrate others' differences and not make them wrong or bad. This is what I want for the world and, sure, it's a big ask. But imagine if we all did it. Imagine if we held that vision, enquired within as to the next best step to support that vision and rallied together as legendary citizens of the world to change it.

A lifelong practice

Why is being our authentic selves a lifelong practice? How come it's not a one-time thing and then, bam, we're authentic all over, Red Rover? Well, like it or not, for the amount of time we have on this planet, our egos, the stories and the in-built personas we have are coming with us. No amount of ayahuasca ceremonies, ego-burning rituals, magic mushrooms, therapy or coaching will ever rid yourself fully from the ego and all it has to say. Sure, there's expanding our awareness through plant medicine, coaching, meditation or whatever helps us create space and distance from our egos, but we will forever be working with them and they will never let up trying on their tricks to stop you honing in on your authentic nature. This is why many feel like they're failing on 'the path' or 'spirituality' or 'personal development' because after each expansion beyond old ways of thinking, doing and being, in time, your wounds, ego stories and deeply grooved automated patterns will be flicked by something or someone, and away you go again.

Back in, I don't know what year, but I'd say I was twenty-five or twenty-six, I was deep in 'the work' but with an immature mindset. I really did think that once 'this' was healed then my life would be peachy. Well, wasn't I in for a rude awakening. I remember going to see a hypnotherapist for a past life regression session. I discovered that in my previous lives there'd been a theme of being 'alone' or cast out by society (sounds awfully familiar in this life too, the going-it-alone part). Anyway, I had such a profound healing and left feeling ah-maze-ing. I truly believed on the car ride home that I was doneskies with my old fight, that I'd finally solved the game of life and healing. L to the O to the L. A few days later those same shitty thoughts returned, those same life-sucking despair feelings were there, and I crashed, hard. I thought I'd failed. I looked at where I was in relation to where I'd been just a few days earlier and thought, *Fuck, I'm never gonna get there, am I?*

I didn't know what 'there' was. Was 'there' happiness? Was it 'peace'? Was it 'rocking life like all the other people I see rocking life who seem to have it easier and better than me'? The standards were high and pre-set by my ego. *If you don't get it in one go then this is never going to work for you.* So, as mentioned, on my personal development spiritual path of immaturity, I set an ego-based goal for myself (not that I knew it was ego based). *Kat, for you to be of service to others outside of nursing, you have to have positive thoughts for twenty-four hours. You aren't allowed one negative thought the whole day!* I wish I could go back in time, pause it, grab twenty-something-year-old Kat by her cheeks and say, 'DON'T DO THIS!' But alas, she did. That me wanted no negative thoughts, no past demons, no wounds that needed rebandaging, no more healing. That me just wanted to be healed. Period. The feeling of being a failure followed me all day, every day.

What I came to realise is that 'there' is not a static destination. 'There' is observing ourselves when we're riding the high wave of life, full to the brim with all the top-notch feelings we can imagine, then watching as the wave gets smaller and the feelings shift a little. It's observing ourselves wishing the wave of life to go back up even though it's going down. Observing ourselves wanting something other than what we have. Observing ourselves down and out, waiting for the next wave. 'There' is staying in observation of ourselves, as often as we can.

This approach is the forever dance and it isn't about living in a 'done' state. We don't want to live solely in the ego state for the time we are here on Earth for reasons that I hope now are glaringly obvious. And we can't live in the state of grace 100 per cent of the time either thanks to the human experience and all that comes with it. We are forever dancing between loving, liking, hating, accepting, tolerating, disregarding, respecting, mistreating and despising all the parts that make us whole. Sometimes you're in the groove of rhythm and blues, sometimes you're cha-cha-ing and you have no idea how to cha-cha. Sometimes you're moving easily and gracefully to sweet tunes, other times you feel like you have two left feet and can't sink into the beat. Welcome to the forever dance.

It's a hard pill to swallow and one that can definitely lead to, *Well what's the fucking point? I don't have all the answers to life and at times it can be so damn hard!* None of us can escape that. No one ever has. We are here, filled with enormous potential, connected with a great source, coupled with the human condition and the heaviness that can bring. If you're anything like me, you'll drop into moments of, *This (life) is bullshit, this is unfair, this is a joke, this is a punishment, this is a curse, this isn't worth it.*

If you do, that's okay, we all tap into that state at different times. Just be sure to not stay there too long, have people around you to talk to and, if you need to, get additional support in how to hold space for that dark place with tools to assist you in staying close to a sliver of light.

Get this tool into your life: Imagine

Just as the professor said to me all those years ago, 'Imagine free, happy Kat and what she looks like, where she is, what she's doing,' I say the same thing to my clients, and now, to you.

I can hear it already . . . 'Kat I don't know how to imagine. I'm not a visual person. I'm not good at that kinda stuff!' You've got to go beyond the locked-in view of yourself and use the power and beauty of your senses to see, feel, hear and know that there is a you; a brighter, lighter, grounded, at-ease self waiting in the wings to come onto the stage of your life and dance in the spotlight. Right now, you're stuck in the deep grooves of who your mind thinks you are and how you have to be. You're trapped in a self that was created for reasons you thought would keep you safe, more likeable, more enough, more perfect, more palatable, more powerful, more tolerable and more in control than your younger selves who, having been wounded by others and life, developed an ego that decided, *Okay, well this is who we gotta be now.*

But that ain't the end vision.

I want you to imagine a you that couldn't be more you if you tried. What do *they* look like? What energy do they emanate? How do they hold themselves? What's their voice like? How do they move through life? How do they approach challenges? How do they show up in all their 'their-ness' to family gatherings, new experiences, friendships and work? How do they treat themselves, speak to themselves and others? If they were a colour, what colour would they be? If they were a sound, what sound would they make? If there was one word to encapsulate them, what word would that be?

Right now, where are you in relation to this version of you? How do you look today? What energy do you emanate? How do you hold yourself? What is your voice like? How do you move through life? How do you approach challenges? How do you show up to family gatherings, new experiences, friendships and work? How do you treat yourself, speak to yourself and others? You get my drift. Where are you at, in the here and now, in relation to the you that is awaiting your arrival?

Now, vomit out all your ego stories about *the real you* who is waiting in the wings. What judgements, fears, concerns, worries and limited views does your ego have about them? Let them out. Leave nothing out. Purge.

Now, find a quiet space to conduct some self-enquiry and ask yourself, *What is my next best step to bring the real me out from the wings and a little closer to centre stage?*

Follow that step.

Meet Clementine

Clementine came to me exhausted, buried in her work, running from motherhood and being present as a mother, and tied to her masculine energy. Joy was nowhere to be seen. Playfulness out the window. Present in her body? Totally foreign. Her childhood had been emotionally volatile, conditional in love and she was modelled to 'do!', to not sit still as 'there's always something to be done'. Her mother found it near impossible to be still and made digs at Clementine's father for sitting around relaxing.

Clementine set foot on the path of reclaiming the 'lost Clems' to piece her authentic self back together. She retrieved her femininity and her ability to be still, to listen to her intuition, to receive support and more. This new way didn't come easy or without a dead weight of resistance. But little by little, bit by bit, she slowed herself down. She put the laptop away when it really didn't need to be out. She played with her daughters. She made banana bread. She watched a movie without her laptop on her lap. She left the house earlier when everyone was asleep to be at one with nature and meditate. She did the little things and as they accumulated over time, eventually she embodied the Clementine that had always been there.

As she settled into her new, authentic way, she and her husband sold their house, took the kids out of school, caravanned around Australia for almost two years and completely dropped *in* to her way of life. She is now in the next practice of coming back home, buying a new property, making more money than she ever has, while being in her feminine. She is coming to terms with the stories and lies she told herself that you can only make money when you're working super hard, a belief she learnt very young through witnessing her parents talk and stress and yell about work and money. She is in the practice of accepting that she can be wealthy, do good in the world *and* be happy. Ego-busting shit at its finest.

Clementine asked herself one good question: 'If I was freed from my mother's beliefs, what would be *my* true and pure belief about money, success and happiness?'

Epilogue

As I write this book, I am thirty-eight years old. The Kat I am today is the Kat my twenty-something-year-old self yearned for. She imagined a better life filled with love, doing what she loves, so well in her being that she glowed and oozed life force. And off I went along the path towards her, crawling, walking, running and dancing along the way, shedding what no longer nourished my soul and loving and accepting all the parts I had shamed. Bit by bit I released what was not right for me, good for me or true for me.

Now, my forty-year-old self is waiting ahead, sitting patiently in the wings, sharing with me what shouldn't be tolerated or taken into the years ahead. That forty-year-old Kat has next-level self-assurance, clarity and spunk. She has next-level wellbeing, mental resilience, intuition, success, enrichment, joy, love, life force and ease. She has next-level 'we ain't gonna fuck with ourselves like we used to'. She is, all in all, unwavering. In equal parts she scares me (well, more like scares my ego) and excites me. And because she (me) scares my ego, it will now send in the resistance army laden with evidence, stories, past situations and all the heavy machinery to convince me 'not to go there' and instead 'stay here'.

This, is the dance.

No doubt, she will have additional core values for me to embody, ask me to sit quietly and make space to connect to her more often, imagine life with *this* layer of authenticity present and what's possible. Well honey, I'm down for the dance, all the while knowing there'll be some major shit storms to weather along the way and ego stories to clear and befriend, yet I still choose to live *while* dying. That truly is *the way*. To keep living into who we are and retrieving the layers of ourselves we've buried *while* we die to the old, the limiting, the inhibiting.

This, is the dance.

The forever dance is to dance with and between our ego and authentic nature, realising that it is not stagnant or static, but always moving. We don't wake up one day and boom, we're authentic now and always. It's a choice. Some moments you'll be dancing closer to the ego and your persona ways, acting in a manner that feels old, odd and outdated in your body. That sense of knowing something doesn't feel quite right is the presence of your ultimate observer, and that's ace. That watchful observer extends the invitation to dance your way home into your true self, and I get it, sometimes the dance ain't fun. You'll want to waltz when the dance is the cha-cha. Or you'll want to hip-hop your way home when the dance should be lyrical. Some days will be tougher than others, and some will be easy-breezy-close-to-beautiful cover girl.

This, is the dance.

Like all good teachings that stand the test of time, there's no quick fix or click-baiting antics. There's no, 'Do this and you'll be healed forever!' Please, be watchful for this in this industry (and many others) because it's used to hook you in, sell fluff and deliver not a lot. I know my message ain't sexy and click-baity and 'in three months you'll be all better and healed', but I tell you, I can't and won't play that game. My values and authentic nature won't have a bar of it. Each day I am presented with products to share on my page for a fee. Unless there is true alignment, it's a 'no'. At the same time, I am turning away money, easy money might I add, but at my core, I know what's right, good and true.

This, is the dance.

You will be presented with 'shiny things' that'll tempt you. This is normal, this is okay. You might play with the idea of taking the shiny thing, or you might actually take the shiny thing, go on an experience and realise, *Shit, that was my ego that made that call.* Or you might consciously know your ego wants the shiny thing, watch yourself take it and know that this is not aligned with your authentic nature. All of the above will take place and it's okay.

This, is the dance.

There'll be people you meet where you'll revert to 'quiet you', or 'over-the-top you', or 'be-smart you'. You'll be standing there watching yourself jump out of who you are and into someone else, and when you're on your way home, you'll wonder why you did that. You'll question if you really 'know who you are' and might get down on yourself, eat shit food and punish yourself in some old, patterned way.

This, is the dance.

You'll have a solid run of being in flow with who you are, feeling so damn good and on top of the world, radiating sunshine out your butt thinking, *Yeah, this is it, this is me, I made it!* And then your car breaks down, your kid is being just a tad more difficult than you'd like, the washing piles up, the workload increases, your partner is not in a great headspace, and you start to feel jacked off. Your flow is interrupted by life and the sun quickly disappears from your butt. You'll stay here in pissed-off land for a bit, wishing the world would go fuck itself, wondering why it's so damn hard to stay in flow . . . But then you'll pick yourself up by clearing the pissed-off-ness, tapping back into the bigger picture, plugging into your values and journalling. You'll receive guidance and the next best step to come back into flow.

This, is the dance.

It won't stop. And if you're disheartened by that fundamental truth, remember this:

What *will* ease up is the amount of time you spend in ego-town stories. What *will* ease up is the time being overcome by ego-town stories. What *will* ease up is the delay between ego-town stories and shifting back into alignment with your authentic self. What *will* ease up is the unrealness and dishonesty game.

You will become a real-time living legend at navigating these two forces within, coming back home quicker, but also, not spiritually bypassing the struggle either. You will uncover new tools and supports along the way to add to your Mary Poppins bag, slowly, surely and steadily placing more and more power into serving your authentic nature over your ego.

As an aspect of our ego story dies, or to be more honest, becomes less powerful and potent, we are reborn and reunited with ourselves. The selves we've shamed, made wrong, been embarrassed about, neglected, shunned and shoved away; we welcome them back to life and let them breathe again. You will continue to meet more of your authentic self along the way. You will collect more of you, claim more of you, love more of you. You will heal more of you, make peace with more of you, and continue to let go of who isn't you. It truly is a forever dance that I beg of you to enjoy! Sometimes it will be a slow waltz, or the cha-cha, or free flowing like a lyrical. At times it'll feel easy; other times, you'll be hard pressed with your back against the wall eating shit for breakfast.

The dance continues.

A pretty well-known Australian celebrity reached out to me on Instagram, wanting to look at how we could collaborate. He asked when I was free for a chat, we made a time and I could feel the ants-in-my-pants kind of energy bubbling away inside. You see, my typical automated response is to please, for I have a deep fear of being rejected and not belonging. My ego pricked its ears, realised what was going on and thought, *Right, I better get involved now. In order to get any deal or collaboration over the line, here's how you have to act, Kat. You gotta be extra smiley, extra available, extra funny, extra flexible, extra accessible, extra cool and anything else that might 'win them over'.*

My ego simply doesn't see that me being me is enough, so it overcompensates by being over the top. I tell you, I am so damn glad that I have this in check now. The days when this part of me hijacked my authentic nature and had me act like a puppet makes me sad. As I type this, I'm imagining myself hugging Little Kat. Gosh, she'd be happy with where we are now.

As I drove to the meeting, I could hear my ego stories, tactics and strategies going off. *Be like this, don't be like that.* For the fifteen-minute drive, I had this narrative playing out. When I parked the car, I unclipped my seatbelt, took a deep breath and asked myself one good question: 'If I were equal to this person, how would I be?' This ego-neutralising question is a go-to of mine when I put people on pedestals, see myself as inferior to them and, as a result, different. My answer: 'I'd be me.' I closed my eyes and quietly said to myself, *Stand comfortably in your own shoes, your own feet and your own body.* This helped me call back the energy that was leaking out and to feel embodied.

Turns out, nothing eventuated with this collaboration, but damn I was proud of myself. I wasn't eager to overplease, give endless options and ideas that were going to burn me out, or say 'yes' on the spot when I wanted to go away and work out if this was a collaboration that actually felt right. I left feeling whole and with my self-love, self-worth and self-respect intact. There are many great feelings to experience in life, but I tell you, that one comes pretty darn close to being in first place.

This very situation took place when my authentic nature was well and truly alive in my life, but the dance never ends. There will be certain people who you will deem more powerful, intelligent, cool or, to put it simply, 'better than you'. You'll be in their presence and wonder why your palms are sweating, why you laughed in a pitch that isn't yours, or why your throat closed over and speaking became near impossible. You'll wonder why you brushed over what you do or don't do for work, why you are putting your partner down and treating them with less respect, or why you're scattered in your energy and behaving like a headless chook.

You might think you're failing at being authentic and beat yourself up about it, but let me tell you right now that you're not, and you don't need to give yourself a hard time. This is an invitation for you to watch, observe and notice your behaviour, take a look at who is in the room, the narrative that's rattling around in your head and how you feel as a result. It's really helpful to break this down after you've noticed that you weren't being you, by getting it out of your head and onto paper.

Who was in the room today?

What was it about them that 'made me' act the way I did?

How did I act and behave? And how did that feel?

What story was I telling myself, the story all the way down to where it hurts?

What part of me needs love, acceptance, to be heard, to evolve?

If I was me in that room today, like *really* me, how would I have been?

The dance continues.

Even after weeks, days, months and years of reacquainting yourself with your self, there'll be times where you won't want to be your authentic self. You won't want to be responsible, account-able, in tune or in check. There'll be times when you'll want to be petty, eager to prove a point at the expense of what could be a wonderful night, petulant or even victim-like. You'll want to give the high road the middle finger and swing right back to ego-land, full of tactics and coping mechanisms that feel familiar.

And just so you know, that's okay.

This is the forever dance.

We are forever twirling, forever cha-cha-ing, forever moving towards new layers of 'us', forever shedding stories that inhibit 'us', forever loving, accepting and welcoming shamed parts of 'us', and forever finding that sweet spot, that home feeling and doing our best to stay close.

Never stop the forever dance because the world needs the real you.

Your family needs the real you.

Your future partner needs the real you.

Your future child needs the real you.

Your future purpose and legacy needs the real you.

And *you* need the real you, too.

To live out who we are while laying our ego stories to rest is the way, the only way, for your real, genuine and authentic self to keep coming alive. Let it breathe in the fresh air, let it bask in the sun's light, let it watch moons rise and walk the less travelled paths of the earth. Let it show you a new way – your way – the way that feels right, good and true for you, all the way home.

Acknowledgements

To Mum and Dad – thank you for never, ever giving up on me and never, ever letting go of the rope. It seems I came into existence to shake up a lot of shit, but to your credit, you always found a way to keep the ground from quaking. Your love was the bell that called me home every time I wandered too far and lost myself.

To Matt – not only are you my big (and older) brother, but you dared join me to face our trauma together. You braced the seemingly never-ending shit storms and side-by-side we squeezed out who we're not, leaving only the best of ourselves to face our futures. Thank you doesn't cut it. This world feels safe and okay because I have you by my side.

To Aunty Julie – my saving grace on more occasions than I could count. Thank the heavens for you and your presence in my life. You knew how to get through to me, how to help me see clearly when I couldn't and how to get to the other side of some of the darkest and most troubling moments of my teenage years.

To Steve – my love. You have invisible pompoms in your hands, forever cheering, 'Give me a K, Give me an A, give me a T!' You have constantly stood by me and behind me, encouraging me to live out who I am and share my heart with the world. Thank you for not being afraid of my pitch-black darkness or intimidated by my blinding light. Thank you for being my person, my rock, my safe place, my love.

To Ally and Mim – my two bonus daughters who have stretched me in ways I never knew I needed, thank you. Without you knowing it, you invited me to face, love and heal many aspects of myself I thought were neatly boxed and tied with a bow. You helped me realise there was more work for me to do and encouraged me to show up with even more 'Kat' present. You inspire me to lead life with authenticity and integrity, to be an example you respect.

To Bailey and Daisy – my fur babies and little shadows. Thank you for sitting under my feet and by my side every day I wrote. Your little nose taps, licks or snores from the couch kept me company this entire journey. You're my angels, wrapped in fur, sent from heaven to make me happy.

To the women in my life, my dear friends – without you, where would I be? You have loved me at every stage of 'becoming me' and that is something I am so very grateful for. To laugh with you, sit with you, cry with you, celebrate with you and do life alongside you, even at times from afar, has and will be something I will cherish until the end of our days.

To my community and clients – your bravery and courage to walk the difficult-but-necessary path inspires me every damn time. Your willingness to go all the way in, shine light on the areas you've hidden from yourself and bring them love, compassion, acknowledgement and tenderness is something I have mad respect for. Thank you for your emails, direct messages and comments that remind me why I do what I do.

To my teachers, expanders and space holders – there have been many of you along my path who have contributed your magic into helping me be me. A very special thanks to 5Rhythms, Elena Pilch, Pete Coles, Jan Beames and William Whitecloud, who have each made a mark in my heart and an incredible impact on my life. Your work, approach and connection to your own selves has profoundly contributed to the woman I am today.

To Professor J – at age twenty-three I came to your rooms a mess, desperate for anything other than the reality I was in. You spoke right to my heart in a way that woke something in me that had been sleeping for a long, long time. You asked me, 'What do you want, Kat?', and I said, 'I want to be free!' Thank you for giving me the invisible prescription to reclaim my freedom. I hold a special place in my heart for you.

To Izzy and Charle – the greatest publisher-and-editor team a woman could ask for. You said to me, 'Kat, give us all of you' and told me to 'dance on the page' with my words. To have you encourage me to be me and not leave a drop of me off the pages meant more than you know. I have cherished every email, every interaction, every comment and every suggestion to make this book what it is. Thank you for honouring it as if it were your own.

To all my younger selves – we made it. Fuck yeah! Now we are home, we no longer have to hide, edit, pretend, bend or please at the expense of our true essence. Little Kat – you can rest, you can play and now finally do what you always did best – dance and sing and light up every room! I love you. Thank you for never letting me forget who we are and who we've always been.

Powered by Penguin

Looking for more great reads, exclusive content and book giveaways?

Subscribe to our weekly newsletter.

Scan the QR code or visit penguin.com.au/signup